With Best Wishes
Christine x

Timeless Poetic Verse

Poems by
Christine Burrows

Front Cover:
Photograph taken by the Author

Notes: compiled by the Author.
All characters and events in this publication,
other than those clearly in the public domain,
are fictitious and any resemblance to real persons,
living or dead, is purely coincidental.

All Rights Reserved.
ISBN-9798308410676

MMXXV

"Christine Burrows"

Timeless Souvenirs

*We measure time by moments that we treasure,
our holidays, our birthdays, Christmas too,
and when we are at home, secure, at leisure,
we plan our time, so that we can pursue . . .*

*adventures in the sun, the snow . . . the world,
our photographs are packed to some extent
with precious moments that we can preserve,
those joys that love and friendship represent.*

*Beware! The time is short, too short for some,
we only have the present to rejoice,
the past is set, tomorrow may not come,
there are no guarantees, we have a choice . . .*

*to make the most of time, use every minute,
as timeless souvenirs inspire our spirit.*

Dedication:

I dedicate this book to my good friend

Angela.

She been there for me throughout my life.

Author's Preface:

This book cotains 240 poems covering a variety of subjects all written in varied formats, mostly rhyming. Some are written in traditional familiar ABAB rhyme schemes, and others are designed in formats created by the Author to include extra internal rhyming assonance. All written during 2024.

Poems composed from a personal perspective about many varied topics to include, love and loss, war and peace, nature, emotions and world affairs. Some pay tribute to special people and some critique life, laws and problematic situations. These poems serve to soothe, disturb, confirm beliefs, challenge ideas, educate the reader, and also entertain. There is a poem here for everyone to identify with.

Life leaves its scar on our heart, and rocks our spirit. We all leave our footprint behind no matter how insignificant we think it is, we are all making history in our own back yard. In all cultures, emotions are universally recognised, no matter who we are, we all have the same basic instincts and feelings. We have regrets, triumphs and lasting memories. We are individuals with opinions. To be human is to err. We make a difference, even when we stumble.

Poetry not only records life, it identifies situations we face. Poetry makes us feel less alone as we are in this life together and face the same, or similar challenges every day. Rhyming words are powerful and can soothe the soul, lift the spirit, excite and infuse the reader with confidence and self-esteem.

Poetry helps us come to terms with sorrow, and encourages us to keep the faith and continue to love. We hope to greet the sun every day with positivity, and if we keep love in our hearts, and believe in human nature, we will live a good life. These poems will reach inside your soul and hopefully touch your heart within, sing to you, and leave a lasting message to ponder.

Enjoy: "Timeless Poetic Verse"

Contents

A Dog Called Snuffy..1
A Life for a Life...2
A Roaring Storm...3
A Star is Born...4
A Sunny Day in Lichfield..................................5
A Tranquil Place..6
A Tribute to Jimmy Carter................................7
A Violent Father..8
Abusive Gene...9
Accountability...10
Add sparkle to Life......................................11
Age is Just a Number....................................12
Ageing Wisdom..13
Another Soldier Lost....................................14
Another Wet Summer...................................15
Arona Skies..16
As Clear as Night and Day..............................17
Atomic Survivors..18
Autumn/Winter Spill....................................19
Avoid Trouble...20
Bargain Hunting..21
Bees Knees..22
Beware the Wolf..23
Black Bird at Dawn.....................................24
Black Dog Days...25
Black Friday Sales......................................26
Blue Bottles...27
Boyfriend Trouble......................................28
Brain Washed...29
Brave Nika Shakarami..................................30
Breaking Vows..31
Brewers Droop..32
Budding Rose Pink......................................33
Bull Fighting..34
Burning Desire..35
Camping Trip...36
Carbuncles..37
Caring for the Environment............................38

Catching Up	39
Catty Sport	40
Cha cha cha	41
Challenging Life	42
Change is Coming	43
Chavvy Peacocks	44
Colin vs Cuthbert	45
Cool July	46
Cricket – A Gentleman's Game	47
Crushed by War	48
Daffodils	49
Daily Exercise	50
Damaged by Life	51
Dead to Me	52
Deathly Lilies	53
Delightful Robins	54
Dementia	55
Doggy Days	56
Early Morning Songs of Love	57
Early Songbirds	58
Ego	59
Erectile Vaccine	60
España Magic	61
Faithful October Skies	62
Fashion Design	63
Fateful Fear	64
Father's Skills	65
Favouritism	66
Feel the Quality	67
Feline Phantom	68
Feline Rules	69
Festive Baking Passion	70
Fields of Poppy Red	71
Finding Peace	72
Flakes of Snow	73
Flimsy Walls	74
Flooding	75
Flying High	76
Foggy Clog	77
Forgiving the Past	78
Fresh Air	79

From Rain to Sun.................................. 80
Gender Prejudice 81
Ghostly Mist 82
Gifts of Loyalty and Support........................ 83
Give to Those in Need 84
Glad It's Over 85
Goodbye to 2024 86
Grief Goes Deep 87
Growing Old 88
Halloween Witches 89
Happy Hoopoe Bird 90
Haunted by the Past 91
Her Autumn Dance 92
Her Loss and Grief 93
High Winds.. 94
Historic Human Nature.............................. 95
Hollywood Smiles................................... 96
Hoping for Sun in June............................. 97
Horizon (The Post Office Scandal).............. 98-99
Horrible Human Suffering 100
Icebound Woes 101
Icy Under Foot 102
If Crows were White............................... 103
Imprisoned Iris................................... 104
In England Where My Heart Resides 105
It's a Dog's Life 106
It's a Matter of Perspective 107
Jealousy.. 108
Judas... 109
July Heat, a Treat 110
June in England................................... 111
Justice is Coldly Served.......................... 112
Keep on Writing................................... 113
Leamington Spa – Where Time Sands Still 114
Leave Behind your Message 115
Lift Up Your Breaking Heart 116
Living in Glass Houses............................ 117
Living in the Moment.............................. 118
Love Grows 119
Love is All That Matters.......................... 120
Lucy Lou Review................................... 121

Maintaining Dignity in Old Age	122
Making Joyful Memories	123
Map Reading	124
March of the Elephants	125
Marmalade Hoverfly	126
Memories of Summer	127
Miners	128
Missed the Parade	129
Mob Handed	130
Moments Remembered	131
Momentous Tales	132
Morning Light	133
Mourning the Special Sycamore Tree	134
Murderous Machinations	135
Musical Nights in Spain	136
My Grandmama	137
My Mog and Me	138
My Mother	139
My Trip North	140
Nature vs Nurture	141
New Bags	142
New Forest Trees	143
New Red Tape	144
Night Flight	145
No Fortune Telling	146
Northern Lights	147
Novichok	148
One in a Million	149
Orange Blossom Bees	150
Pacing Time	151
Passionate Easter	152
Passionate Release	153
Peace at Night	154
Peaceful Halloween	155
Pensioners are Sitting Ducks	156
Performance of the Sun Flowers	157
Phantom Fog	158
Phone Scamming	159
Pink Mallow Bindweed	160
Postman's KNOCK	161
Procrastination	162

Propaganda	163
Pumpkin Puns	164
Pure Graceful Swan	165
Recollections	166
Red Veined Darter	167
Reflections of Yesterday	168
Remembering Dean Kuch	169
Respecting Thy Neighbour	170
Retribution	171
Romancing	172
Royal Blood	173
Sahara Sand	174
San Eugenio	175
Sea Dogs	176
Seasonal Madness	177
She Smiles	178
Silver Boots	179
Silver Swan	180
Soaked to the Skin	181
Some Never Find Happiness	182
Songs of Love	183
Spanish Bureaucracy	184
Spiked Habit	185
Spring and Summer Life	186
Spring Reviews	187
Spring Serenade	188
Stay Calm	189
Stealing from Nature	190
Street Lifers	191
Stylish Iris	192
Summer Gardens	193
Summer Gardens Speak to me	194
Summer Lane	195
Summertime Joys	196
Sunday Afternoon Driving	197
Surf the Wave	198
Sweet Revenge	199
The Canarian Storm	200
The City Girl Grew Wise	201
The Final Journey	202
The Law is an Ass	203

The Misery of Rule.	204
The Mushroom Cloud	205
The Poet Writes.	206
The Puppeteer.	207
The Ref	208
The Tree Fell Hard.	209
The Trial Man	210
Timeless Poetic Verse.	211
Tinnitus.	212
Trashy Food	213
Trashy Tash	214
Trashy Wedding.	215
Tree Hug.	216
Tree Surgeons Save the Day.	217
Trial by Media	218
Trials of Life.	219
Trick Treat.	220
Uncouth Wives of Beverley Hills.	221
Uncovering the Truth	222
Under the Blue Spring Sky	223
Unladylike Behaviour.	224
Unpredictable Life.	225
Vernon's Crusade	226
Virtuous Spirits.	227
Vociferous Rage.	228
Vulture Culture	229
Walking the Dog	230
War Torn Syria.	231
Warring Words Die Hard.	232
Water Striders.	233
What Makes Someone a Hero	234
When Looks Can Kill.	235
Windy Days	236
Winter's Menacing Chill	237
Youthful Fashion Trends	238
Youthful Memories.	239
Author's Biography.	240
Nature Inherits the Earth.	241

"Christine Burrows"

A Dog Called Snuffy

A Labrador they all adored was welcomed to the home,
he learned so very quickly, he was not allowed to roam;
he cowered at commands from his old master's heavy foot . . .
this frightened pup was shaking after blows impact his gut.

He always wagged his tail, was friendly to the little girls,
they made a fuss of him, and he would quell all their concerns.
This household pet was well behaved, a joy to have around,
but he was always scared of boots, that dealt a mighty pound.

For Snuffy was abused, and he would squeal in pain when kicked,
his owner was an angry man and when annoyed, he flipped;
and unbeknown to others, he was suffering in pain . . .
internal were his injuries that he could not sustain.

One day he could not walk and he would stumble to the floor,
he wanted to go wee, but couldn't make it to the door;
this was the final kick that was to break this doggy's back,
and lying on the kitchen floor was Snuffy, that's a fact.

The owner made excuses, hit by cars within the fog
and tears were shed by little girls who mourned their lovely dog;
but looking back they knew the truth, the dog was kicked to death . . .
by someone who was violent, and took his final breath.

"Christine Burrows"

A Life for a Life

A life was lost, to pay the cost,
another man would die,
a tragic loss, and now the law,
is bold and never shy.
Their paths were crossed and blood was spilt,
a day he can't forget,
and everything would change,
as there is sorrow and regret.

If only he had walked away
from conflict when it rose,
he would have saved himself from strife,
but threats he chose to pose.
Now silence falls upon the cell,
where he believes he'll pay . . .
a sentence full of dreadful hell,
or worse, he'll die today.

A Roaring Storm

A roar was heard above my head, a clap, a slap, a crack!
The noise alarmed a cooing dove, and ducks refused to quack.
A streak of white electric light then sparked across the sky . . .
as fear ran through my veins, I ran for shelter to keep dry.

As tiny drops of rain began to speck, as if they're drawn,
I knew the storm would drench the trees, the flowers and the lawn.
The burst would soak the town, then blessed us with a special scene
of colourful design, a rainbow soothed with its routine.

Behind the houses and the church, I glimpsed this special show,
reminding me that nature has the gift of rain and snow,
and when the sun decides to shine, we praise the season's glory,
but when the showers won't relent, it is a different story.

"Christine Burrows"

A Star is Born

A gentle wind has caught her hair,
she had so much to give and share;
when strolling in among the trees
her spirit rests upon the breeze.

With angel wings she soars up high,
as butterflies now dot the sky;
for she is welcomed to a place
where faith and hope is full of grace.

We say goodbye, and see you soon,
and when we gaze upon the moon;
we will remember every smile . . .
and cherish every single mile.

Farewell to this sweet natured child . . .
you will be missed, as you beguiled,
a star is born to shine above . . .
to bring to others all your love.

For Abigail, who died just 10 years old on 9th March 2024.
She battled with cancer, and she will be greatly missed.

A Sunny Day in Lichfield

The warmest sun caressed the trees, the teasing breeze has gone,
so close and thick the atmosphere, beneath a scorching sun.
The birds have lost their singing voices, not a word at dawn,
in cosy nests the heat increases, wooden twigs are warm.

The cloud has cleared, the sky is blue, the heavens beat with heat,
as summer came a tad too late for bees to gain a seat;
but butterflies still flutter, and the flowers are in bloom,
and I will wear my shorts before the rain has chance to loom.

And on a day like this, my happiness has found its song,
and filled with jubilation, I begin to dance along . . .
as I'm infused with inspiration, steps increase their stride,
and I may skip into the park, as I enjoy the ride.

A Tranquil Place

Keep inside a private place
where only you can be alone;
Sweep it clean of all disgrace,
and smelling of fine sweet cologne.

Never let another know
you have this inner core of strength;
cleverly you'll not let go
of this internal sturdy stealth.

Only you can recreate
inside your mind, a pretty scene;
loneliness will not translate
into a valueless routine.

Calm and tranquil interlude . . .
will soothe chaotic troubled times;
palms and flowers ease your mood,
and fill your head with rhythmic rhymes.

A Rimaric, a poetic form created by the author

A Tribute to Jimmy Carter

This democrat was once disgraced,
he never stepped out of the race,
he rode the storm, did not confirm
and met his troubles face to face.

He championed our conservation
pardoned dodgers in the nation;
adversaries were met with smiles
but did he quell the world's inflation?

Whatever he did, he remained
withstood the scandal, never stained,
and now we laugh at false confessions,
indiscretions truly famed.

But here he is as large as life,
unscathed by battle, and of strife,
he lives and counts one hundred years,
and hasn't since betrayed his wife.

James Earl Carter Jr was an American (born on 1st October 1924 was a Politician and humanitarian who served as President of the United States from 1977 to 1981. He was a member of the Democratic Party.
A scandal broke out about his extra marital affair which he denied.
He died on 29th December 2024 before this poem was written.

A Violent Father

His raging anger turned his face a fiery crimson red,
this bully hurt his daughter as she lay inside her bed;
as it was time to go to school, and she would not wake up,
she screamed and cried each morning as the drama would disrupt.

And in defiance she decided not to rise each morning,
the cycle of abuse continued, she was not conforming—
distressing was the scene, as these events were hard to see,
as soon as she was able, she would take the chance to flee.

And witnessing the fury as the temper rose so quickly,
will traumatise her siblings as it left them feeling sickly;
and no remorse was ever shown for this brutality,
this father had no shame and absent was morality.

As violence within the home becomes a threat to health,
it physic'lly and mentally will drain all of your strength;
and no one knows how it will scar the memory for life,
a childhood where such violence haunts nightmares every night.

Abusive Gene

It is their true belief that women are the slaves of men,
behind the scenes they toil, and prejudice will rise again . . .
suppressing those who never chose to be intimidated,
inside the dark there is no light, they're crushed and subjugated.

Have men forgotten who it was who gave them life and love,
the nurturing and caring, Mother's warm protective glove.
Alas the domineering gene, where ego has been fed,
encourages a man to be abusive in his bed.

Accountability

Acceptance of one's action comes to mind,
Communicating culpability—
Consideration, left behind to find
Occurrences of liability.
Upending lies, so truth can see the light,
Negating those who have been innocent;
Tenaciously we set our stall to fight—
Affording blame for every incident.
Believing in some justice when a crime,
Insists on causing harm to other souls;
Liaising with the law, report on time,
Imposters often hide beneath the stones.
Together we can forge a moral code—
Yes liability should be exposed.

An Acrostic Poem

Add Sparkle to Life

I pop the cork, and tilt my glass, and pour this buoyant kiss,
I watch the great eruption of this magic liquid wish;
and celebrate the frothy life, this bottle has within,
I share this chilled and naughty beverage that's full of sin.

I taste the sparkle on my tongue, the zing that clings inside,
the tiny bubbles spring and ring, and downwardly they slide;
the liquid tantalises with its popping sunny flair,
and when I drink this Spanish treat, it always takes me there.

I clink, then raise my glass and drink to my arrival home,
the effervescent dancing fizzes with a joyous foam;
that carbonated, scintillating, vibrant, lively zest,
that never fails to lift me, and admonishes my stress.

Age is Just a Number

I never thought I'd be this old,
although my thoughts are made of gold,
I keep up with the latest trend,
and on technology depend.

And keeping fit is how I cling . . .
inspired by life when it is spring;
as time moves forward, never back . . .
to keep on moving down the track.
Please make these moments last a while, I need to take it in,
the sunny day, the warmth in May, to hear that violin.

Alas, my fast advancing years
will never slow, or quell my fears,
the speed in which the hours still pass,
where days soon fall into the past.

My mind's made up, I'll stop the clock,
and take my time when at the dock
to watch the ships sail on the sea
and let my spirit set me free . . .
I'll breathe in all that fresh sea air, and feel the breeze within,
allow my wings to fly up there, with birds I'll take a spin.

As moments spent outside myself,
where I am young, and time is wealth,
will soothe my journey, fill my soul
with happiness to make me whole.

Ageing Wisdom

When in a world where youngsters rule,
the elderly maybe uncool . . .
behind the scenes they pull the strings,
as they have seen so many things.

Their wealth of knowledge, wins the show,
so much they've learned, so much they know,
considered sometimes slow, infirm,
but youngsters have a lot to learn.

To reach a ripe old age on earth,
is sometimes down to luck of birth,
and choosing healthy paths to walk,
know when to act and when to talk.

So never underestimate,
a man or women in debate
who shows the signs of ageing scars,
as they can see beyond the stars.

"Christine Burrows"

Another Soldier Lost

Untimely death, we mourn the loss,
a casket polished with a gloss—
we grieve beside the solemn grave,
our eyes were wet for this young brave.

The grief, it settles in our heart,
and it will never leave, depart;
forever will our Mother cry—
she cannot say her last goodbye.

Dissolved before she had a chance
to love, to take a second glance,
the sadness rises like the shame
no war can be a welcome game.

The pain will never leave her side,
in no one can her love confide,
as all was stolen, now bereft,
no culprit for this petty theft.

Another Wet Summer

The fine rain soaked my hair and skin,
I felt the moisture deep within,
my bones were oiled, each moistened drop,
would soak with every plop, plop, plop.

All day the gentle rain fell down,
the flowers glistened in the town,
my specs were full of flecks of mist,
I couldn't see how I'd been kissed . . .

by water falling from the heavens . . .
leaving stylish round impressions.
Finest rain would soak my hair,
the frizzy look, beyond repair.

And once at home, I stayed indoors,
I never ventured to the stores . . .
I languished in the warm and dry
and cursed another wet July.

"Christine Burrows"

Arona Skies

The arid atmospheric, as the sun is beating down
upon the sandy dry terrain, a desert in the town;
with irrigation, populations flock to scenes like these,
a civilised and cultivated island ill at ease.

The rocks of age command the space and nothing moves a mountain,
as pipes are laid above the ground to make a pretty fountain.
Oh yes the sun is shining, and the tourists get a tan,
there is no rest inside the night without a whirring fan.

The local men build tirelessly to keep the island running,
machines are working day and night, I often hear them humming,
and I appreciate the toil of every working soul,
without these loyal workers, I'd be left outside to boil.

The desert sand clings to the cloud and sweeps across the sky,
I see the white cloud sullied by a dirty sand supply;
the grains fill up the atmosphere so that we cannot breathe,
a problem man can never solve, this island's ill at ease.

Although the Canary islands are well maintained, as local workers tirelessly toil to keep everything moving, nothing can solve the problem of the Calima.

A Calima is sand held in the cloud overhanging the islands in the Canaries and the atmosphere causes breathing problems for humans, and many tourists are hospitalised whilst on holiday.

As Clear and Night and Day

The silence of the night begins to close my weary eyes,
and into dreams I fall to wallow in your sweet surprise,
as visions of the past can sometimes haunt and please at once,
if only I could see your face when morning light confronts.

The long and quiet hours through the darkest roads I've been,
return to me when I allow my mind to drift and dream.
The entrails of the past where history cannot be changed,
begin to be much bigger, and can never be contained.

Until the dawn clears all the obstacles within my mind,
and I remember all the good things, when my thoughts unwind.
I feel refreshed, renewed and ready for the day ahead . . .
until the sun begins to fall and takes me to my bed.

Atomic Survivors

The day was warm, they heard a cock'rel cry,
and willow trees were dressed in skirts of beauty,
the sky was blue, a plane was flying by,
as workers left their homes to do their duty.

A flash of light grew bigger from the ground,
and rose into a mushroom cloud above;
the vacuum sucked the life from all around,
as fusion liquified remaining love.

As hearts were charred, and flesh was stripped from bones,
and human nature vaporised and melted;
as life evaporated on the stones,
in seconds devastation was selected.

The endless sadness of annihilation,
would leave its mark inside the souls of those
who live with memories of degradation,
when colour drained from every single rose.

The epicentre, now a grave of peace,
where spirits speak from oleander trees;
the voices can be heard, they often speak,
of instant death among the Japanese.

Now cherry blossom trees replace the cinders,
democracy has opened up their hearts;
Japan has prospered, healed are all those splinters,
their thinking concentrates on peaceful arts.

The lesson learned is harsh, without a curfew,
in war we mourn, it steals our human virtue.

"Timeless Poetic Verse"

Autumn/Winter Spill

As winds blow hard and leaves now fall,
installing cooler days . . .
this Autumn phase now tells us all
that rusty gold displays,
prepare us for the freezing chill
with heavy sighs,
those cloudy skies
will tantalise
when snow complies
disguising rooftops with its spill.

The Chime Operandi, a poetry form created by the author.

Avoid Trouble

For every action and reaction, consequences rule,
mistakes are made and sometimes temper can take time to cool.
When faced with tense and shaky situations, watch your step,
and learn to bide your time and not react or interject.

When feathers have been ruffled, and someone has lost control,
a silent moment quells the storm, if tongues don't wag too long.
As lessons learned in this regard prevents the escalation,
and we avoid the sorry shame of fateful confrontation.

Bargain Hunting

A shopping trip to lift my mood,
I can't relax, I must be shrewd,
as bargain hunting is a task
that I decided to unmask.

The rules are easy, watch and learn,
I need to pay some close concern,
to pricing up in every store,
ensuring that I don't pay more.

The market always has us marked
as fools when using shopping carts,
so be aware of tactics used,
or your last penny is abused.

Be smart and be aware of scams,
as they will scupper all your plans,
be wise and shop with confidence,
your purchase has a consequence.

So find a bargain, be clued up,
a gem is hiding in the rough—
that dress price has been high and bold,
now slashed in half, and worth your gold.

"Christine Burrows"

Bees Knees

I'm chilling in the clover, buzzing with my tiny wings,
and landing even slower, pollinating little things;
on carpets finely textured, richly woven into life,
as spring is never questioned, I am living without strife.

My mission is my mantra, and my dedication, key,
a little bit like Santa, as I swear to guarantee . . .
delivery of nectar, as us bees are very keen,
I am a bloom inspector, and I'm working for my Queen.

My dancing, slow and steady, as I'm energised by faith,
sometimes I feel unsteady, as some flowers are unsafe;
so if you see me hiding in a rose, I love the view,
I find it quite exciting, tasting nectar's sweet fondue.

"Timeless Poetic Verse"

Beware the Wolf

Now the wolf wore the fleece of a sheep,
his deception was really quite cheap,
he raided the pen,
and ate every hen—
whilst the farmer was still fast asleep.

Black Bird at Dawn

As the dawn remains silent and still,
and the sun has the will to bring light,
I am stirred from my sleep by the thrill
of a black bird deposing the night.

He is hopeful and sings from the heart,
and he brings such a tuneful repose;
as this tranquil, sweet musical start
beats the sound of those murderous crows.

And the skill of this bird in a black feathered coat
has a will to be musical with every note.

Black Dog Days

He told a tale of sorrow, as his woes had dragged him down,
no hope in his tomorrow, when his mood renewed his frown.
no optimistic outlook when depression grips within,
as coping with the swinging blues stole every bit of him.

When thoughts consume, will not abate, the numbing chills the heart,
and one by one his closest friends would very soon depart.
Alone, despair controls a life that once was bright and cheery . . .
descending into dark black cloud is sad and dull and dreary.

There is so much we have to learn about the mind of man,
where some are full of joys and others fall without a plan.
No matter how much help one gives, the answer is the same . . .
we have a choice to make life good, if only we can change.

"Christine Burrows"

Black Friday Sales

The day arrived with all its pride,
to buy until we drop!
with sales to tempt, they have supplied,
another way to shop.

Personified one day this week,
as Friday has turned black . . .
as retailers have found us weak
we cannot turn our back.

They offer discounts for one day,
the flock begins the hunt,
attracted to the fine display,
with bargains to confront.

But I will not be so enticed,
I'll keep my pennies safe,
until those prices have been sliced,
I'll keep out of the race.

Blue Bottles

Tenaciously they buzz buzz buzz in coats of neon-blue,
the word is out to target food, I've witnessed quite a few,
and when they gather, chattering, they're sociable it seems,
but in my kitchen they produce some loud and scary screams!

Contaminating everywhere, they spread disease and germs,
I much prefer them outside when attacking wiggly worms;
so colourful and wonderful, a pity they're detested,
and when they buzz around my head, they make me feel molested.

As bottles like a piece of meat that's bloody raw and off,
they suck up all the contents when you're dead or sleeping rough;
they love a smelly den where all the animals are kept,
but if they fly too close to me, my swat will intercept.

Boyfriend Trouble

The mood had changed, she felt a chill
that marred her joy with morbid skill;
anticipation of those words . . .
she hoped his mood had false concerns.

But when a rumble starts to sound,
as it becomes so very loud,
and when he spilled the beans that day . . .
her heart would pay in every way.

The morning sun was not so bright
as cloud would enter with its blight;
and deaf she was to her poor friend,
no empathy she did extend.

The hours slow when gloom consumes,
and dull were all her afternoons;
although she knew the end had come,
the reasons all began to strum.

And as the days beat over time,
she realised that her decline
was never worth the price she paid,
for she was always in the shade.

And moving on to see the sun
means heartache can be overcome--
there is a sea of fresh new faces,
waiting for this girl's embraces.

Brain Washed

Do we believe what we are taught,
when we're allowed to think?
When dominated by control,
can breaking chains still link.
The freedom to decide may be,
a burden in the end,
when let free from the lions cage,
with words that can be penned.

And realising lies were told,
and we believed them too,
will unhinge our reality,
as nothing seen was true;
for eighty years a brain was washed,
with treachery and fear,
until the spell was broken and,
once blind, all views are clear.

A Grandmother who finally escaped from North Korea to South Korea with her three generations of her family, was taught to hate the Americans. The children are taught a song from an early age referring to Americans as (American-Bastards) When she was finally helped by a group of American journalists to escape to the South, she realised that she had been fed lies all her life.

"Christine Burrows"

Brave Nika Shakarami

It took three men to beat this girl, just sixteen years of age,
so frightened were they of her power, she had so much rage;
her bravery, her courage brought these men their biggest challenge,
fighting other men was easy-- women? Far too gallant!

These cowards, yellow-bellied men, these sissies were afraid,
they met their match, as this young girl was far too bold and brave.
This bright and vibrant flame of life would have to be put out,
as fire spreads and power would be far too wild to doubt.

And face to face with women who are powerful and tearless,
intimidating each of them, for they are far too fearless;
the only way they coped when such a mighty strength exists,
was in a gang of three, to kill a potent force like this.

They beat, abused and hurt her flesh, her spirit was preserved,
she fought until the bitter end, this treatment undeserved.
But they were fearful of this girl, she dared to question men,
this pretty flowering petalled rose was crushed by three of them.

These murderers went home to wives and put their kids to bed,
and none of them knew what they'd done, and nothing more was said;
the shame of blood was on their hands, to hell they all will go,
as justice will be served in time, and only God will know.

Nika Shakarami was an Iranian teenager who was sexually assaulted and killed by three men working for Iran's security forces. One man molested her whilst he sat on her. She fought back, kicking and swearing. The men then beat her to death with batons. This was all because she refused to wear the veil (hijab).

Breaking Vows

Together with a prayer to share, these lovers made a home,
and they enjoyed the company, and did not feel alone.
When their eyes met, their love was set to be one made in heaven,
in time their anniversaries accumulated seven.

Alas they grew apart, blindfolded was their eye to eye,
and tears were shed, in desp'rate cries, as love had walked on by.
The future sadly lost appeal, their hearts had failed to heal,
diverted was their focus, as this wagon lost its wheel.

Those eyes were searching for a change, betrayal sang its song.
and bitterness would end this love, and neither thought it wrong.
Not every marriage has the will, to honour its survival . . .
foundations here, not built to last, this love, had found a rival.

"Christine Burrows"

Brewers Droop

When the calories turn into fat,
and libido is low and it's flat,
give up on the beer,
a stiff will appear . . .
and your sex life improves after that.

Budding Rose Pink

With bravery, tenaciousness, the bud reached out to drink . . .
revealing perfect petalled splendour, washed in hues of pink,
she spread her wings beneath the rain, to soak and quench her thirst,
until her vibrant leafy skirt was buoyantly coerced.

Her beauty was beyond compare, she yearned to share her smile,
so hungry for more admiration, wildly fluttered style;
and to her heart, the bees were drawn, their love was evident,
attractively she bobbed her head, her fashion relevant.

Her youthful dance accompanied by other blooming friends,
she was the star, she would go far, her beauty never ends.
The summer sun and gentle drops of heavenly fine mist,
would rest upon her petals pink, as if she had been kissed.

The weather took its toll and her fine velvet robes were soiled,
the edges turned a rusty brown, her smile was soon destroyed.
Her energy was sapped inside, her pretty head would droop,
and newer buds took centre stage, she aged within her group.

Ne me quitte pas, Ne me quitte pas, my love for her defended,
she heard my whispered plea, but her debut had surely ended.
Her youth was gone, her wrinkled face was almost dead with drying,
she took her time, her leaves once moist, were shrivelling and dying.

I captured in a photograph, her stunning presentation,
she gave us all a pleasing show, with faithful dedication.
I'll not forget her summer smile, her open hearted rise,
this youthful rose, with perfect poise, was passionately prized.

(Ne me quitte pas) means: (Don't Leave me)

"Christine Burrows"

Bull Fighting

The mood was exciting, the crowd wanted blood,
we heard the bull moaning, his hooves made a thud.
The Matadors line up in sequins and frills,
with swords and with daggers displaying their skills.

They wave a red cape at the bull as he comes,
inciting the beast in a charge, as he runs;
he's fooled and distracted, and he cannot win,
the dagger strikes deep as it enters his skin.

The odds are against, and the bull will not know,
there is no escape, he is there for the show.
The battle commences, exhaustion prevails . . .
and soon the sharp object reveals his entrails.

The bull will be destined to be meat for tea,
at least he can battle whilst he is still free;
tradition is something the Spanish will boast,
they play with the bull, before killing the host.

Bullfighting is legal in Spain to this day, although some cities have shunned it. In Madrid they still practice this barbaric display before killing the bull.

Burning Desire

The moth flew far too close, the flame had singed his flimsy wings,
now flightless, he's remote, his days would end, he sleeps with Kings.
The boundaries are pushed until they break and crack with age,
and love may not survive if we don't compromise, engage.

The bird will never fail to sing, at dawn he lets us know,
in earnest he will spread his wing, to let his love bestow,
his loyalty until he dies is evident in nests . . .
the bird displays reliability, he does his best.

We give our heart in hope that someone cares for our desire,
and if our love has failed, we may allow it to retire.
We sometimes suffer grief when we fly too close to the flame,
remember that a love that's pure has power to remain.

Camping Trip

The bugs, the hugs, the warming mugs
the sleeping bags, the lads, the stags;
the noisy crows, a world that slows,
around a campfire, friendship grows.

And lying down to face the sun—
with stars and moon, at one become,
a break from city life maybe
a place where we are free to be.

Appreciate the great outdoors,
adventure means our feet have sores;
we're cooking on an open fire,
on busy days, we soon retire.

Now looking back, the fun was good
we hid inside that quirky wood;
survived among the wildlife where,
they didn't mind us being there.

Carbuncles

My ageing skin is breaking down as lumps and bumps appear,
the moles and freckles make their mark and nothing here is clear.
Within the folds the sagging rag, the derma swings about,
it won't spring back, the skin is slack, to creams I am devout.

Is that a spot, or is it rot, my skin decays with age,
I keep it clean, but sun is mean, and burns my face with rage;
but years have mounted on my pelt, there's nothing I can do,
I want to tie my skin up tight to make it look brand new!

Alas, I have decided that my skin is weather worn,
I've used it for so many years, and sometimes it's been torn,
but most of all it holds in all my bones and muscles too,
my heart is grateful to my skin as on my sleeve it grew.

"Christine Burrows"

Caring for the Environment

For those who have the privilege to walk the earth today,
creating history and marking life with what they say;
I am the keeper of my diary of many words,
to spread my song each dawn just like the varied tuneful birds.

And everywhere I look I see a new and troubling thing,
and change reminds me time is moving forward with its swing.
My eye is keen to watch and listen, feel and touch the day,
to trust my instincts when I feel the yearn to get away.

We can't escape the forward march into the future zone,
we live inside the past sometimes, and reap what we have sown;
Our step right now will matter, the effects will recherché
controlling our behaviour will dissolve the disarray.

To be informed, recycle waste and use less energy,
be careful what you purchase, as there is a penalty;
each saving may be small, accumulated, it transforms,
and teaches children habits that ensure those new reforms.

Catching Up

The sun is low and shadows form,
It's not yet June, but it is warm;
my step it quickens under sun
until my walk becomes a run.
And heading home to find you there,
    your smiling face,
    so full of grace,
    as months have past
    time fled so fast,
and you have much to tell and share.

We hug and kiss, it's you I miss,
we talk at once, work through the list;
and nothing stops exchanging views,
I listen to exciting news.
We share some tea, just you and me,
    and time flies by,
    we care not why . . .
    we sip our cup
    whilst catching up.
A pleasured meet, we both agree.

Catty Sport

Behind the privet fence he lurks, two eyes intense and keen,
not seen by anyone, invisible in his routine.
The night is black, no moon to brighten corners of the garden,
and looking for his prey, he is determined not to pardon.

Then suddenly a mouse decides to run across the field,
a piercing scream releases, as this stalker is revealed;
a leap, defying gravity, is one of his great gifts,
his sharp extended claws are ready for a killing blitz.

He pounces on the target, as he always hits the mark,
and blood is spilt, there is no guilt, relying on the dark.
The victim, taken by surprise, this panther is so slick,
triumphantly he keeps his prize, this butchery is quick.

Cha cha cha!

When challenged to the cha cha cha . . .
I took my partner's hand and smiled,
performing steps . . . a superstar,
my swinging hips had soon beguiled,

I moved across the floor, and soon . . .
the rhythm took my feet again,
and to the tune I swayed and swooned
until the audience of men . . .

began to cheer with sheer delight--
I couldn't stop my dancing shoes,
was flying high and in full swing
as I enjoyed my great reviews!

Challenging Life

The wilting rose reminds me
that true beauty never lasts,
we dwell on pretty moments
that soon melt into the past.
I mourn for yesterday,
yet I look forward to the future,
with promise of some peace,
with just a touch of silly humour.

Alas the changes challenge me,
as they shape diff'rent scenes,
and nothing stays the same,
they often sabotage dreams.
Surrounded by my memories,
my history is long,
and when I'm gone,
I'll leave behind,
my happy little song.

Change is Coming

Our thoughts will turn to Halloween,
as summer ends and in between
the holidays and Christmas fun,
another celebration's won.

With pumpkin magic, golden hues,
I will be wearing warmer trews,
I'll say goodbye to sunny days,
when entering the cooler phase.

At least our cosy beds at night,
will help us sleep without a fight;
the rain will come with wind attached,
when flowers die, and bees are snatched.

I'll keep some summer in my heart,
appreciate the golden art
when trees begin to change their tune,
and bare their branches to the moon.

My outlook will be positive,
as dormant gardens fail to live;
I'll see the changes, welcome calm,
revitalise my favourite psalm.

Chavvy Peacocks

These chavvy girls sat silently, a posing pout or two,
with plumped up lips, and lashes sweeping up and down on cue.
In baby pink, their trackie pants had clung to curves in places,
and when they spoke, their accents left a smile on certain faces.

Their fingernails, like weapons, sharp and pointed, patterned too,
beware if one of them was pointing straight in front of you!
They didn't miss a trick when showing off designer bags,
with labels hanging out to tell us all to raise our flags.

Their padded breasts pushed out their assets, cleavage was their thing,
a nest of hair to make a bird believe it was still spring.
Stiletto heeled white trainers put discomfort to the test,
and strutting out upon the stage, they did their very best.

And queuing up to board the plane in flats and baggy trews,
a plain old bird with peacocks showing off their pink tattoos,
I sipped champagne, relieved that I still blended in with those
who didn't give a damn about the clothing that they chose.

Colin vs Cuthbert

When Cuthbert was born there was envy and scorn,
the gauntlet was thrown for a fight;
but Cuthbert was young, and his loose tongue was strong
and Colin soon fled from his sight.

They both went to court and a battle was fought,
could Colin beguile with his fame?
The judge would soon rule, as this dude was no fool,
though he knew his good looks were to blame.

They stood firm on all legs, these pillars of strength,
hell-bent on surviving each other;
and when the Judge spoke, as he was a good bloke
these two soon became bosom brothers.

And so it was said, that these pillars were led,
by a mission to be enemies,
but when all's said and done, the brotherhood won,
on birthdays, there were reveries.

For both these sweet cakes, were such excellent bakes,
with a chocolate coating real thick;
but it's Colin for me, he's delicious you see,
M&S is by far the best pick.

M&S is a popular upmarket store in the UK called Marks and Spencer. They sell food and clothing of high quality. They invented a chocolate birthday cake called Colin the Caterpillar. A rival food store called Aldi invented a similar cake called Cuthbert the Caterpillar. M&S took Aldi to court to try to stop Cuthbert from being manufactured. The court ruled in favour of Aldi and they were allowed to bake Cuthbert without any restrictions.

Cool July

The sky is unpredictable and cloud is full of woe,
the sun has failed to stop the droplets falling down below.
With rain and cooler climes, July has been a disappointment,
if summer sun won't shine this time, there could be an annulment.

No bees or butterflies are seen, the nests of birds are cold,
if only skies would let the sunshine beam with streams of gold.
Alas another day will pass without a sunny ray,
and all my summer dresses will not see the light of day.

Please let the heat beat down and treat my skin to glinting sun--
to warm the earth and let the caterpillar have some fun,
allow the wildlife freedom to rebirth, enjoy July,
before the autumn winter months begin to make me cry.

Is it too much to ask, to let an English summer dazzle,
and buck the trend of rain, and let a dry spell scorch and frazzle?
To send a wave of heat to us, so we can dance with glee
before we all forsake the north to find a warmer sea.

Cricket - A Gentleman's Game

A gentleman's game, the ashes they claim,
a win for the team with a run;
when in eighty-two, Australia won,
the mourning of loss had begun.

The men dressed in white, put up a good fight,
the loss was a smear on their name,
since then English players, have toiled in their labours
to master this gentleman's game.

And leg before wicket, will forfeit their ticket,
to gain accolades with success;
defending positions in rainy conditions,
is often not easy, at best.

The Aussies have sun, to win a home run—
we English give balls a good spin;
as cricket is ours, we keep all the stars,
and letting them win is a sin!

The term (Ashes) was first used after England lost to Australia at the Oval in 1882.

The Times carried out a mock obituary of English cricket, saying the body of cricket had been cremated and the ashes were taken to Australia. This inspired the sporting public and (The Ashes) became something the British had to defend. Despite all this hype, India still remain the best teams in the rankings.

"Christine Burrows"

Crushed by War

This country, like a cultivated garden,
was prospering and free to live in peace . . .
the flowers grew as colourful as tartan;
diverse and special, overlooking streets.
This jewel with its gem shone like a star,
but evil eyes with envy spot the lights;
and like a star, in danger from afar . . .
the jealousy is murderous . . . excites.

A daisy chain of innocence and joy,
the people had no will for war or conflict;
yet bullies have propensity to toy . . .
and flick a cigarette-- light up the district.
A heavy boot then stamped upon the flowers,
tore trees from roots and made a fiery grave;
and bombed the houses and the high rise tower . . .
until they flattened everything they'd made.

Destruction, demolition, breaking hearts
all tantamount to crushing human spirit,
and all the time the man in charge remarks . . .
he has the right to grab-- there is no limit.
A scene of war, with relics of past life,
a sunset with its innocent twilight,
the tombs of debris built by bitter spite,
as soldiers execute both day and night.

There's nothing left, the land is scarred and barren,
no joy, no laughter, nothing but a pit;
a graveyard full of ghostly souls that happen
to haunt this place and never will submit.
Our history lies in the broken stones . . .
how harsh and hateful man is to his brother,
and in the ashes lie decaying bones,
in grief and sorrow, war makes mothers shudder.

Dedicated to Ukraine

Daffodils

A field of yellow heads prepare to let the sun and rain
come sprinkle nature's magic with the season's keen campaign—
and in the distance I can see the bobbing dots of colour,
as pretty ladies hover over fields with wings that flutter.

A wave of yellow dancing bonnets float upon the breeze,
against an em'rald sea, supporting spring-like nominees;
and every petalled sunny face delights our watching eyes,
as daffodils begin to host a special sweet surprise.

And nestled in together on their stalks they all conform
a proud and perfect plethora of daffodils perform—
the show of sunny flowers in a field once dull and barren,
is filled with yellow pigment from a palette full of passion.

Daily Exercise

The whirring sound of rolling roads brings comfort to my ears,
the clanging metal dumbbells sing with power, bringing tears;
the body workout thrives and strives to rip those muscles tight,
the thumping pumping exercise is moaning on alright.

The gym pulsates with music, and the reps are on the beat
the battle lines are drawn, and many fight to feel the heat.
To reach our goal and stay in touch with mind and body moves,
We're slaves to our routines as when we're fit our life improves.

I like it best when I've achieved the target for the day,
I leave with beaming smiles, my happiness is on display--
as bodies need a challenge and the exercise is key
to keeping bones and muscles tight and functionally free.

Damaged by Life

A fragile soul, a life of hardship, evident in deeds—
abused and damaged all her life, her garden full of weeds.
She never smelt the flowers, sensed the beauty all around,
and so her life was damned by all the hell that she had found.

A damaged heart and body, no control of anything,
and so her hate was focused on exactly the same thing.
As what we learn as children is not easy to forget,
behaviour will repeat, and they themselves become a threat.

How do we stop the cycle of abuse of children here?
A blind eye will ensure that this continues, it is clear.
But on the other hand, we can't excuse such dreadful acts,
and being vigilant will mean that we report the facts.

Dead to Me

I stumbled on a letter that you wrote when you were mad,
and it revealed your truest self, and reading it was sad;
the message I received inferred, there was to be no "we",
I didn't get a mention, yet the mail was sent to me.

Your messages were all about demands upon my time,
with what you needed, what you wanted, taking what was mine.
I often felt I was a child, manipulated too--
and pleasing you, a duty, serving you, and only you.

The cold and calculated theme was always evident,
you thought yourself too mighty to be kind, benevolent.
The pedestal you set yourself was high above the rest,
the mediocre tend to think they are the very best.

And cleverly, deceitfully, your sword would cut and carve,
a swift blow to the head to warn-- the blade was very sharp.
The serpent's tongue would lash with venom, every time it spoke,
recipients would duck and dive, the poison always choked.

Alas it seems you seek the adulation of your friends,
but no one is now listening, your thoughtlessness offends;
your weak insipid ventures just reveal a lonely soul,
where you cannot survive unless you have complete control.

I very quickly learned to navigate your selfish mind,
exposing you for what you are, the egocentric kind.
I saw a monster in my midst, a brute without a heart,
and looking back I am so glad that we are now apart.

Deathly Lilies

Reaching from the depths of destitution,
lilies know there is another way;
never giving up their restitution,
daring to breathe life into display.

Out of canker, lilies bring great beauty,
sinking roots beneath the murky mire;
hope and faith becomes undying duty—
blooming loyal beacons to inspire.

Dying lilies putrefy and fester—
death decays the flower given time;
memories will linger as they pester—
loss of life will die inside the grime.

Never to forget this life endeavour,
symbolising souls that part forever.

"Christine Burrows"

Delightful Robins

When Robins make their nests in trees,
they wait until the Winter freeze
has thawed the breeze with sunny days,
when flowers colour grey displays.

When earth below has loosened buds,
they peep above the frozen rugs . . .
as wiggly worms aerate the soil
and turn the earth with earnest toil.

Returning from their holiday,
the Robins sing now it is May,
as love is in the air for Spring . . .
the mating season's in full swing.

The leaves on trees will cover nests,
to hide these love birds with red vests,
and through the summer reverie,
the Robin bobs above with glee.

When Autumn leaves begin to fall,
the Robin might be very small . . .
but flying to a warmer clime
will save this little bird of mine.

And those who stay behind will know
that there will be a fall of snow,
so leave your seed for Robin dear . . .
in Winter he will persevere.

Dementia

Corroding cells depleting in his head,
before his body knew, his mind was dead.
Awake, but not quite there to share the truth,
the past has gone, no knowledge of his youth.

And those around intensely grieve for him,
their Father, keeps his secrets deep within;
an empty life, repetitive and small,
where memories refuse to reinstall.

Alas, that spark is lost behind the eyes
a cerebral extraction that belies
connections that are broken without vi'lence—
now sunken in an unforgiving silence.

Invisible this power set to freeze,
inside the grip of terrible disease—
as life is real, no chance of a rehearsal,
dementia will delete, without reversal.

"Christine Burrows"

Doggy Days

Dogs,
they satisfy a human need,
love's guaranteed with loyalty,
because they always aim to please,
they make us feel like royalty . . .

with wagging tails they greet and meet,
on hind legs stand to nab their treat.

A Peppered Pickle, is a poetry form created by the author

Early Morning Songs of Love

The silence of the early morn,
at dawn when life is still;
I witness on my lawn,
a blackbird with an orange bill.

Before he sings his pretty song,
I long to hear his tune,
he forages along
a patch lit by the fullest moon.

And when the silence breaks, I hear
the cheerful chirping sound,
to me his plea is clear,
this bird, by loving thought is bound.

The Octahex, is a poetry form created by the author

"Christine Burrows"

Early Songbirds

The Early bird has cheerful song,
he sings along with glee;
and frees his melody so strong
in tuneful perfect key.

The moment when the sun appears,
my inner fears are gone;
here comes the bird, he perseveres,
his potent chirp has won.

I wake up to the sound of life
all strife subsides within;
I pin my hopes on birds who strive,
to not forsake their kin.

Ego

When ego builds a pedestal up high,
and looking down, the drop below is steep,
the egotist may even start to cry . . .
as selfishness incriminates the weak.

The guilt may seep into the bones and freeze,
destroy all self-esteem, and knock their faith;
when elevating, heights begin to tease,
as shame can turn them red, when losing face.

So let your climb be slow, don't cheat your friends,
integrity will bring its own rewards;
consider every word to make amends,
as honesty will win its own awards.

When ego takes a fall, it has no limit . . .
disgrace can steal the heart and kill the spirit.

Erectile Vaccine

The bloke was blown high upon acid,
his member's performance was flaccid
his mistress was keen
to get a vaccine
to rapidly pump up his asset.

Espana Magic

This beach is full of oily bodies brown and nicely tanned
where shadows of the palms are painted on volcanic sand;
the gentle waves upon the shore are crystal clear azul,
between the rocks, the crabs enjoy a warm sea-water pool.

Torviscas is a place where sky is blue and sun is hot,
and sangria is served with fruit and berries on the spot;
where tapas is consumed with friends, and smiles are spread around—
and strings will echo tunefully as guitars will astound.

The joys of Spain are colourful and vibrant is this life,
a holiday beneath the sun will take away your strife—
and you are welcome when the sun gives way to evening moon,
when dancers bring their magic, in a tapping shoe platoon.

"Christine Burrows"

Faithful October Skies

Reflecting streaks of colour,
set behind our sacred church.
The spires are standing proud,
as they are pointing up to search;
a moment when the sun inspires
us all to look and see . . .
as every eye,
is free to view
this pretty jubilee.

The moving cloud sweeps clean the sky,
allowing beams to shine,
the blue and orange contrasting
in magical design.
The darkness soon descends
upon the town,
the show is over,
and captured on my phone
is just a moment
in October.

Fashion Design

I sew before the fading light, and fight, until I finish,
although mistakes along the way . . . ambition may diminish.
But I refuse to let it go, until my efforts win . . .
as giving up's not in my soul, the task gets under skin.

Unpicking, sewing, changing reels, it steals my time for sure,
my efforts may not win the day, but trying is the cure.
Then finally, euphoria has filled me with such glee . . .
a masterpiece emerges, and it is all down to me!

I proudly wear brand new design, as I know I'm admired,
a mix of colour magic, and a pattern that's inspired!
As sewing is my passion and creating, is my muse,
when I invent the newest trend, receiving good reviews.

Fateful Fear

A tingling wave of squeezing knots that grip the stomach tight,
and everywhere you look there is no respite from this plight.
A chilling terror can consume, alarm bells blare despair--
a phobia unleashes fear and demons will impair.

The horror shakes foundations and will always numb the brain,
anxiety replaces calm and dread will leave a stain.
The scream within is loud and bold, as inwardly we're stunned,
inside we try to be composed, stability is shunned.

The eyes reveal the panic, as foreboding fills the soul,
and once the fear has taken hold, there is no real control.
When laboured breathing starves the heart, collapsing our defences,
hysteria will wildly launch, as fateful fear possesses.

Father's Skills

My Father built a clock and it stood tall inside the hall,
the pendulum would tick with time and never did it stall;
his engineering skills came handy, fixing everything,
from squeaky doors to broken drawers, his skill was in full swing.

Electrical, hydraulic, he invented many toys,
a rocking horse for adults, was another of his spoils.
He painted pretty scenes, the Laughing Cavalier was fine,
reviving broken objects with a touch of new design.

When he fell ill, relying on the doctors for a fix,
he realised that flesh and bone and hearts that didn't tick
would be an area he wished he'd concentrated on,
as he could not get well, he realised he'd soon be gone.

The day he died, the kettle broke, the clock had stopped in time,
the door lock would not open, and the bell refused to chime.
The house had paid respects to him, declining to behave,
and all the objects he had fixed, went with him to his grave.

Favouritism

To keep the peace, and quell the tide
some people carry too much pride . . .
that puts a strain on all the rest.
because they think they are the best.

This preferential accolade . . .
when others shine in each parade,
yet they don't win the prize, but see . . .
the same one winning in this spree.

The privileged are winning here,
as in this water, crystal clear
a name is highlighted in pen . . .
as favouritism cheats again.

Discrimination segregates,
with bitter words, it isolates;
and when the facts are penned in ink,
we see the stain and smell he stink.

An unfair system is to blame,
as sometimes rising up with fame
means who you know, not flair you share,
we see the evidence right there.

And I suggest that we expose
how flawed selection has arose . . .
when talent shines, it needs no prize,
as everyone will use their eyes.

Feel the Quality of Life

Alone she walked along the path, the silent wood was still,
she heard a rustle in the trees, the crows had no good will.
Then suddenly a butterfly just kissed her on the nose,
and from the depths inside her heart, her happiness arose.

She turned the corner where the park was full of screaming kids,
she realised they could not keep excitement under lids.
The joys are always there to see, if eyes are keenly fixed,
when life throws up some challenges, and trips us up with tricks.

The positive will line the cloud with silver and with gold,
appreciate today, protect your heart against the cold;
and never cast aside an opportunity to smile,
as wisdom means we bring some joy to every single mile.

"Christine Burrows"

Feline Phantom

The neighbourhood's in disarray,
a stray cat on the hunt;
he hides by day to catch his prey . . .
so clever was his stunt.

He flushed out mice with his affront,
a blunt and callous act;
he got results with his conduct,
so quick was his attack.

In fact he had a great impact,
this cat had cleaned the street;
his fame intact, the mice were trapped,
they couldn't stand the heat.

Discretely he had found his feet,
completely vindicated;
this fete he often would repeat,
and he soon integrated.

A Metrical Echo is a poetry form created by the author.

Feline Rules

The keenest eyes you've ever seen,
he masters streets outside;
with time to spare to clean and preen,
to hold his head with pride.

And hiding where he can survey—
to keep an eye on things,
and with command he can convey
that he belongs with Kings.

Intruders on his patch beware,
a lesson taught out there—
this feline friend will never share
as he controls what's fair!

This predator will outwit most—
intuitively eager,
and never think that you can boast
an insight that is deeper.

His curiosity has power
finding what is true—
with many lives he tests the hour,
including me and you.

And when he lies beside the fire
and purring at your stroke—
manipulating hearts desire
convinced he gives us hope.

"Christine Burrows"

Festive Baking Passion

The shiny tinsel means it's time
to rhyme some words of faith;
and I'm inclined to stand in line
to buy a Christmas cake.

I wake at dawn, decide to bake,
I'll make it with my hands;
and I will rake and I will take
some bits from many lands.

From Chile almonds fit the bill
I fill my grinder tight;
the icing will be made with skill,
a snowy white so bright.

In India the fruit will win,
I spin my wooden spoon;
and mix within the bowl of sin
a drop of brandy swoon.

One slice of cake is filled with spice,
It's nice with cups of tea;
and my advice is short, concise,
when sharing cake, you'll see . . .

that you'll make many friends, it's true,
as queues will form outside;
so make your debut, bake anew,
and share your skill with pride.

A Metrical Echo is a poetry for created by the author

Fields of Poppy Red

A sea of floating specks of red,
are winking in the breeze;
this speckled field of pain and dread,
not one man will be freed.
The innocence of flowers that
contrast with bloody hands,
where lambs behave like tigers
and a bullet changes plans.

Among the waving flags of pretty
flimsy wings of red,
these boys would view the scene, serene,
before they'd all be dead.
The sorrow touched our hearts
as war is callous, cold as stone,
the injured bled, no tear was shed,
as they all died alone.

Finding Peace

A peaceful Sunday morning with a sunny sky of blue,
will fill my heart with hope that there will be some peace for you.
As lately anxious thoughts have crowded every single thought,
allowing deep depression to consume with no support.

My wish is that you can relax, enjoy a summer's day,
and read a book to introduce another way to stay . . .
without the need to run and hide and hibernate this time,
the panic that engulfs, and can control your state of mind.

Alas, I see that scary look, the fear I've seen before,
and soon you have to leave, I see you packing up once more;
escaping from yourself, when there is nowhere else to go . . .
I hope that over time you will feel peace inside and glow.

Now locked inside your castle where no one can come inside,
the walls are high with very little light to be your guide;
if love can soothe your heart, then you can let go of the pain,
enjoy the sunny sky and see those rainbows after rain.

"Timeless Poetic Verse"

Flakes of Snow

Snow,
with flakes of perfect crystal white and new . . .
the flurry blew against my garden fence;
and slowly, paint was splashed upon my view,
was magically creamed with its intense.

And when the moon beams bounced upon the scene,
the glitter sparkled, everywhere was clean.

A Peppered Pickle is a poetry form created by the author

"Christine Burrows"

Flimsy Walls

There was an old man from the sticks,
who built a house minus the bricks,
when a breeze blew it down,
he's the talk of the town,
his honour could never be fixed.

Flooding

Torrential pour from cloudy skies, the deluge soaked the earth,
it drowned the flowers and the flies, all creatures were submerged;
the bursting rivers overflowed, the water crept inside,
the residents were then employed in ebbing tortured tide.

The drench was swift, it washed the grass, and soggy was the ground,
and those who thought the rain a gift, now cursed cascading sound.
It did not stop for days on end, until the flood took hold,
and plunged the town into a swamp, the spout was uncontrolled.

The rescue . . . slow, and sunk below were all their prized possessions,
they learned to swim, wet to the skin, and there were no exceptions;
foundations water-logged for days, the draining took its time,
and what was left, was ruined by the muddy oozing slime.

Flying High

Hang on tight and don't let go,
we need to fly up high you know,
speed is of the essence here,
exciting is this chandelier.

Swinging from it may be mad,
but flying high just makes me glad,
feet are lifted off the ground
pay close attention, I expound!

Timing may be paramount
be careful if you have some doubt,
board this saucer if you dare
and you'll be lifted in the air!

"Timeless Poetic Verse"

Foggy Clog

Fog,
intensifies and clogs the scene,
with its routine to blind our eyes,
the cloggy mist was unforeseen
and on the lower ground it lies.

A dewy drizzle swamps the lawn,
and it won't clear before the dawn.

A Peppered Pickle is a poetry form created by the author

"Christine Burrows"

Forgiving the Past

When growing up at home, she was not safe,
as violence was something to avoid;
her Father ruled with fear, there was no grace,
whenever he was angry or annoyed.

Her sister suffered at his cruel hand,
encouraged by her Mother every time;
no mercy shown and tears you understand
were frequent, as this treatment was a crime.

She had her dreams, was eager to fulfil
a life where she'd be free to choose in peace;
to wake without a raging heated spill—
and listen to the birds sing in the streets.

But she forgave her father for his sins—
he never learned about her great achievements,
or knew his Grands and all their special wins,
because he instigated disagreements.

And looking back her life was very good,
she learned to not let bullies rule your life,
as she escaped, and always understood—
protect yourself from those who give you strife.

Fresh Air

We always love to breathe the air
and dare to share the atmosphere;
the breeze that teases flowing hair,
without a care, we leave our chair
to go outside and fill our lungs,
and let our noses breathe in tons.

We crash about, we are devout
to working, searching, never doubt . . .
that air is there, a lot about,
and even if we start to shout,
there's always air, our hearts desire,
to help us breathe in every hour.

So why do people smoke, pollute,
their mission is so resolute;
the pain of it is quite acute
and chokes me with its disrepute.
No longer is the air so clean,
and stealing it is really mean.

As chimneys, cars all bellow smoke,
I need a mask or I will choke,
the engine that exudes a coat
of carbon black with every stroke,
is killing everyone-- I swear,
we need to breathe in clean fresh air!

"Christine Burrows"

From Rain to Sun

The early hours before the dawn
the storm outside disturbs,
an English curse again is born
I'm torn by tempest bursts.

The pitter patter never fails
to wet the pavements it impales

and clouds of grey are everywhere
to scare and taunt the crowd . . .
if only shrouds of dull despair
would rarely be aroused.

***** ***** *****

The thumping sound of stormy days
betrays my thoughts of sun,
I'm overcome by my malaise,
when rainy phases stun.

Then rainbows shine with colour hues,
they take away my bitter blues . . .

a break from rain now lifts my mood,
and soon, when I awake . . .
upon the lake a glint tattooed
I view a sunny shape!

A Pinned Decimal is a poetry form created by the author

Gender Prejudice

When clearing out my Mother's house, I found her secret box,
'twas hidden out of sight, beneath her bed with double locks.
I found the keys inside her drawer, where she kept precious jew'ls
I took the key, and opened it, to view some broken the rules.

At first I saw a photograph, my father in his youth,
I looked into this cold man's eyes and recognised abuse,
and searching further, letters swore of love eternally . . .
and disappointment of a birth, the first born child was me,

A girl, when he had begged the Lord, to give him just a son,
but here I was, a girl, not knowing what there was to come.
The box contained a bonnet and some tiny little mitts,
assuming that the clothes were mine, my heart was torn to bits.

When I grew up and married, I was soon to have a child,
I cared not for the sex of it, as I was so beguiled,
And looking back I didn't have the chance to prove myself,
to show my father I had gained his talents and his wealth.

My father died before his time, he had so much to give,
we went our diff'rent ways as I had so much life to live;
he said that he had no regrets, I know this was not true,
my father looked into my eyes, saw everything I knew.

The past is done, he kept his bitter gender prejudice,
his heart was closed to any woman who would talk of this;
he lost the chance to know his girls, as there were three of them,
all worth their weight in gold, with much more talent than most men.

"Christine Burrows"

Ghostly Mist

The ghostly mist has kissed the sea
and soaked the atmosphere;
a blanket filled with mystery—
effects of it severe.

I cannot see the town below,
the palms have smoky lofts;
as fog has clung so very low
the tourists now have coughs.

The temp'ratures have soared so high,
the sticky heat is glum,
and high above this misty sky,
is oven warming sun.

But in my mountain cave retreat,
it's cool and dry and clean,
and from my rooftop comfy seat,
I feel like I'm a Queen.

When the Canaries are being challenged by high temperatures, the extreme heat creates a ghostly mist that sometimes settles on the lowlands and on the sea early in the morning. It looks mysterious and threatening.

Gifts of Loyalty and Support

When wise men help us see the light,
by teaching us what's wrong and right;
I listen, learn and guide my step . . .
avoiding those who are inept.

I witness selfishness and greed,
as those who steal more than they need,
will feel no shame, and line their nest,
and fail to see the treasure chest.

Possessions don't bring happiness,
but caring actions, I confess . . .
will bring a smile and touch my heart,
as thoughtfulness is filled with art.

The smallest gesture lifts my gloom,
and in such moments I'm consumed;
when loyalty, support exists,
I'm grateful for these special gifts.

Give to Those in Need

We never know the path we'll walk,
or whether dreams come true,
when born with optimistic hope,
that life will be good too;
we see those people on the street,
they're begging for a cent,
and even when they're old and grey,
I see their discontent.

As life's unfair, we learn to share,
and give to those in need;
we see ourselves, as life compels
us all to plant a seed.
Humanity sets us apart
from animals and birds,
be generous to those who live
in very diff'rent worlds.

Glad it's Over

I saw you standing there, bewildered by your situation,
brought about by your own hand, and your insinuation.
Decisions made, now diff'rent paths, the two of us would take,
without a single word, you left, but my heart did not break.

I knew, one day, that you would leave, no loyalty on show,
and guarded was I, as deceit can throw a bitter blow;
relieved was I, the time had come, I knew just what to do,
my love for you was over, and my strength would see me through.

I always felt alone whenever we spent time together,
as times were hard and I did not enjoy the stormy weather.
Now memories are stale, and they no longer haunt my sleep,
as I've decided you were just another selfish creep.

And what I do not understand, is why you contact me?
Relationships when over, mean you stay an absentee.
And where you are, or what you think, or if you're full of woe,
whatever you are feeling, I have no real need to know.

Goodbye to 2024

We say goodbye on New Year's Eve,
the past is set in stone . . .
when looking back, we laughed and grieved,
but we were not alone . . .

as poets share a unique gift,
our words that tell a tale . . .
the joys and sorrows sometimes lift
when sharing each detail.

Our rhymes may resonate and stay,
emotions spill with tears,
identifying every day . . .
with many inner fears.

The ups and downs, when we look back
have forged a bumpy journey;
but on the whole we've kept on track,
our stories have been worthy.

Grief Goes Deep

I cannot know another's grief,
emotions can go deep;
I know that sorrow is a thief,
as loss can steal our sleep.

We dwell on memories to soothe . . .
to help our lonely path,
the bumpy journey, never smooth,
abandoned aftermath.

We learn that life is all too short,
and death is short and quick;
relying on our friends support,
who battle with the sick.

The end will come for all of us,
we lend a helping hand,
as sometimes life can be unjust,
subsides in grains of sand.

Priorities soon change when we
are lost inside such grief;
and linking hands with you and me
is always very brief.

"Christine Burrows"

Growing Old

I never thought I'd grow this old,
with extra folds of wrinkled skin,
this sin of age may curse my gold,
as years accumulate within.

I never thought I'd cross the line
and lose my mind and memory,
I see now that old age maligns . . .
my good looks now are history!

I never thought I'd be infirm,
as bones confirm my stiffened gait,
and I'm too late to catch the worm,
as sleeping in has made me late.

I never thought my legacy
would also leave behind my words,
affirming in my poetry,
a lifetime of my wise concerns.

A Seasoned Octet is a poetry form created by the author.

Halloween Witches

The witches vow to stir the pot,
to stop the girls at play
they have an evil plot
and cast a spell to make them pay.

They fly on broomsticks late at night,
excitement in the air;
on Halloween ignite
a fire to boil their potion there.

To tempt the children with a treat
a sweetened drink is made;
and falling for deceit
their consciousness will surely fade.

And captured are the innocent,
by venting witchery;
the sorcerers content
to damage our society.

The Octahex is a poetry form created by the author.

"Christine Burrows"

Happy Hoopoe Bird

Sporting proudly wildly, soundly,
crowned on head, with feathers spread;
zebra white and black, are loudly,
colourful, but feared it's said.

Hoopoe birds foretell . . . disturbing,
watch and learn, demonic turned;
reputation undeserving . . .
omens may suggest they're spurned.

When I saw this fella walking,
landing by my feet so shy;
looking at me, he was a stalling . . .
dropping by, to just say hi.

If you are lucky, you will see this bird walking along busy streets, in the Canary Islands, as they fly in from Africa.

It is said that if a hoopoe bird lands near human habitation, it is a terrible omen of disaster or even a death, but as we know folklore is just a myth. You will be amazed at this bird's beauty close up.

Haunted by the Past

He faced some inner turmoil,
with his shifting ardent mind,
as selfishness was paramount,
he was sometimes unkind;
tormented was he by himself,
he would not open up,
and often missed the happiness,
with only half a cup.

He ran away to clear his head,
as thoughts would cloud his view,
and those who were so close to him,
did not know what to do;
forsaking them, they lost their faith,
and he was all alone,
if only he would mend his ways,
he would be welcomed home.

Alas he never saw the light,
his candle burned so low,
and everywhere he looked,
he saw the sadness come and go;
his memories were dogged by
sad events he could not change,
he lived within a bubble
and outsiders thought him strange.

Her Autumn Dance

She danced beside the water's edge,
her branches stretching upward.
Nothing stopped this fine parade,
her full skirt flamed with colour.

Making her debut, no longer coy . . .
but confident and proud,
this was her moment to shine.

All year she had waited
to free her passion for autumn,
her beauty was beyond compare
as her leaves turned vibrant orange,
to share her glee . . . belated joy,
she delighted her audiences.

And other trees allowed her lonely show
to take a bow, a tribute to this blushing bride.
Young and innocent, flamboyant and charming.

She twirled for one last time . . .
before she joined the throng
of naked trees.

Her Loss and Grief

I felt the pang of sorrow, when I saw her tearful eyes,
her secret grief would never leave, there was no compromise.
Consumed by darkness, even on a sunny day, she grieved,
no smiles, or cheerful laughter, would encourage a reprieve.

The days turned into months and she still mourned the day he died,
she never noticed time was swiftly passing, as she cried.
All joys within her garden, where the roses faced the sun,
were all dismissed as futile, as her lover would not come.

The early morning lark was busy getting on with life,
whilst in her world, she squandered time, when held within this strife.
Not able here to function, morbid was her long malaise . . .
until there was a glimpse of light, when music washed the greys.

Although the songs reminded her of moments long ago,
it lit a flame of happiness, as memories would glow,
and soon she felt him near, her heart was open to his touch,
and in her dreams she visioned him, and grief no longer crushed.

And when a new day dawned, she saw that life was here to share,
with nature she identified, as seasons changed out there.
She let the sun warm on her skin, and felt the summer deep within,
appreciating little joys, she felt her anguish wearing thin.

High Winds

The wind blew hard and flapping flags
were ragged with the gust,
all leaves were blown about,
and trees were undressed by the thrust.
The tirade cleared the pavements,
as no man could stand the force,
as speeds of up to ninety miles
an hour, were endorsed.

The draft had found its way beneath
my door to chill the bone.
I corked up all the gaps to stop
invasion of my home.
It stripped the final petals from
the stems of every rose,
the strong and forceful wind had grounded
all those noisy crows.

Historic Human Nature

We hang onto the past as we're secure in its firm anchor,
relentless in its truth, it will not change its final answer.
The past still, it will not shift, there are a few regrets,
we always learn from ghostly memories and silhouettes.

The good, the bad, may haunt, but history can still repeat,
as naive souls will never learn how humans can mistreat.
Technology advances, and can rule our daily life,
but we are flawed by treachery, with warring words of strife.

When crossing swords with enemies, our anger knows no bounds,
we kill, we maim, no remedies can quell those human sounds--
the fight to be supreme, the selfish traits of human kind--
will mean that we subdue all those who try to cross the line.

To live in peace and harmony could mean the human race
will lose its sense of purpose, as we fight for every space.
The battle will continue, as our progress will not stop--
and when our temper rules the roost, the world outside may pop.

"Christine Burrows"

Hollywood Smiles

Those cheesy veneers are on show with a grin,
and does this confirm they are joyous within?
When teeth gleaming white are displayed with such pride,
I wonder if smiles hide a frown deep inside.

The stars are adept in promoting their pleasure,
the language of smiles makes us envy their leisure;
perfection is never so flawless it seems,
as writhing inside is a mood full of screams.

And those who can smile with a toothless display,
with genuine joy, they exude and convey . . .
there is no pretence, there is light in the eyes,
authentically honest, without a disguise.

Hoping for Sun in June

The chilling air can't help but share, and touch my skin with cold,
in June when I expect the square to be caressed by gold;
instead the sun has disappeared, the ground is damp and soggy,
although the birds appear with cheer, my mood is vague and groggy.

There is some hope, as weathermen are promising some fun,
before our June has slipped away, we hope to feel the sun.
In England where it rains all day to soak our garden flowers,
and too much water tends to stay in puddles made by showers.

My dream is that I wear my hat and dress next week for sure,
when I can strut in warmer climes and be more self-assured,
that I will not be rained upon by constant skies of cloud . . .
I'll wear my sunnies, sandals too, and brighten up the crowd.

"Christine Burrows"

Horizon - The Post Office Scandal

The Local Office for the Post, it never makes mistakes—
computers they've installed detect and monitor disgrace;
and all the staff accused across the country . . . every man,
arrested by Police for theft, to prosecute . . . their plan.

And sent to court were Postmasters, and sentenced to the crime,
so many of them held account, each one of them declined;
and subject to the law, this new Computer fooled them all,
as none of them were guilty, but each one would take the fall.

Discovering Horizon had a fault, it made mistakes,
and decent men and women were accused and in disgrace;
authorities resisted and would not admit the fact—
that they'd discovered problems, and they would refuse to act.

The battle took its toll on those who suffered at the hands,
of men who were dishonest and would not divulge the scams,
they covered up this big mistake, because of their deceit,
and with the Office for the Post you just could not compete.

The tables turned, as scandals such as this, would be exposed,
a case was brought to court to show Horizon diagnosed . . .
the system was still faulty, unreliable erratic,
and what the victims suffered was destructive and traumatic.

"Timeless Poetic Verse"

NOTES:

The British Post Office is a Government organisation, and a law unto themselves. They are allowed to bring prosecutions to the court without the involvement of the Police. No member of the public can fight against them. If the Post Office computer reports an employee for stealing money, no one can contest it.

The British Post Office Scandal is sometimes also called the Horizon Scandal, because their computer was installed in all Post Offices. It was discovered, subsequently, that the computer falsely created shortfalls in the accounts of thousands of sub-postmasters.

Between 1999 and 2015, more than 900 sub-postmasters were convicted in the courts for fraud, false accounting and theft, all based on the Computer data from Horizon owned by Fujitsu. It was proved that employees at Fujitsu could remotely access computers at any given Post Office and change their figures. They were constantly, manually, correcting errors made by the system. This was kept a secret for a very long time.

Many sub-postmasters were forced to pay for the shortfalls that they were not responsible for! All this money went into the profits of the Post Office. The criminal convictions, imprisonments and the loss of homes, livelihoods and debts were too heavy for some, and the toll on victims' families led to illness, stress, divorce and at least four suicides.

Eventually a case was taken to the high court in 2017 for 555 sub-postmasters led by Mr Bates in a group action against the Post Office. A court settlement of £58 million for the victims only equated to £20,000 each.

After 20 years, all those who were wrongly accused, had their convictions overturned in court, and they all received compensation in the region of £400,000 each, from Horizon. It has been described by then Prime Minister, Rishi Sunak, as one of the greatest miscarriages of justice in the history of the United Kingdom.

Horrible Human Suffering

A world where human suffering, continues to be bold . . .
and not because of weather woes or freezing bitter cold,
or soaring heat, or lack of food, or absence of a roof,
what I reveal is suffering that has no real excuse.

The mean regimes around the world where leaders rule with hate,
with torture and with threats of death, abusive rules of state . . .
denying people freedom, to curtail their every move,
to stifle all their passion, as all hope they will remove.

Injustice and corruption has a tendency to win,
in places where dictators bury secrets on a whim.
The lies and treachery will leave a trail of blood and bone,
as tyranny will sanction with its bitter undertone.

Icebound Woes

When icicles adorn my house,
they sometimes fall, and spike a mouse;
he squeals with pain and runs for cover,
and as he does, there falls another!

As prints are left upon the snow,
a bird will hop about and know . . .
there are no worms this time of year,
but still they look and persevere.

My car will need a kettle hot,
to thaw the freezing windscreen spot,
I dig a path to free the way . . .
my car would much prefer to stay.

The night is still, the winter chill,
has kept all pets inside until
they need to go, as nature calls,
returning with their snowy paws.

Icy Under Foot

The yard is strewn with leaves and debris,
wind has tossed up dirt,
no longer is it warm
and all the flowers have been hurt
by heavy rains and frozen stains
that killed the roots with frost,
and creeping over hills and valleys,
winter's hand has glossed.

Reflecting sparkle on the holly,
berries shine and gleam,
the chilling biting atmosphere,
is bitter and its keen;
it's time to say goodbye,
escape to southern warmer shores,
before the snow hides grass of green,
and frozen ice explores.

If Crows were White

Would we think crows were murderous if all of them were white?
Associated feathers black have added to the spite.
The darkened deeds embedded in appearance, tell a tale,
would we be so judgemental if the crows were light and pale?

If loving doves had darker coats, would they not be so dear?
Those feathers pure and white depict a bird we think sincere.
Would views about behaviour change, if doves were black not white?
As I suspect beliefs about these birds is not quite right.

Appearances deceive us as all birds can be accused
of ganging up and punishing, as many birds abuse;
fallacious folk have blackened crows and tainted them with horror,
the truth is that a dove can kill, despite its fairest colour.

White Crows and Ravens do exist, but seeing them is a rare occurrence. Also there are black doves too.

"Christine Burrows"

Imprisoned Iris

What was your crime dear Iris? You are fenced in by a wire.
Is this because of jealousy, this beauty we admire?
I see your pretty purple petals, waving flags so bold,
and want to free you so that you can flutter all your gold.

Alas, you're held to ransom, just because you're standing tall,
but I still hear your plea, and know your plight is never small.
I see some budding blooms have flowered way beyond the fence,
and freed themselves to show the petalled beauty they dispense.

The deep rich colour on display has given me great joy,
a unique frilly skirt is always twirling, never coy.
I am reminded that in spring you smile at passers-by,
I wonder why the wire fence was built so very high?

In England, where my Heart Resides

I want to feel the breeze that teases with its forceful blow—
and see the twirling brollies from my high rise down below,
to walk the cobble stones where ancient Royals trod in mud,
and breathe in Merry England where my heart is understood.

To see the spires, and view for miles, the magic of their faith,

the flow'ring posing roses waiting for my warm embrace;
a market scene where men are keen to sell their fresh sweet plums,
and shops where volunteers have smiles for everyone who comes.

I'm touched by warm nostalgia when I see St Mary's church,
and in the parks where robins sing to praise the silver birch.
As absence makes me fond of all those magic scenes of home,
when I return, I'll celebrate, and vow to never roam.

As England holds the key, she unlocks all of my desires,
as soon as feet are on the ground, she reignites my fires.
But most of all, those smiling faces, greeting with their fun—
excites my inner child, as every single heart I've won.

"Christine Burrows"

It's a Dog's Life

A dog is so intuitive, with them you can't pretend,
and even if you're ugly, they will always be your friend;
they all have faithful hearts, and unconditionally love,
their loyalty goes to the grave, to Heaven up above.

A dog will know your inner thoughts, and they can smell your fear,
instinctively are drawn to smiles, appearing so sincere.
With no regard for how you're dressed, or whether you are clean,
once they have made a bond with you, you'll be their King or Queen.

To earn a treat, they'll walk the beat, and jump through many hoops,
run miles to find the ball you threw, protect you in disputes.
And never will you be alone, on dogs you can depend,
a faithful friend for life, a dog will be there 'till the end.

It's a matter of Perspective

When tragedy begins to filter through and gnaw our bones,
we look for blame to counteract those heavy weighty stones.
A scapegoat found, it is profound and charges soon are levied,
and in the court, a sentence sought, with venom it has merit.

As accusations thrown about, can stick to us like glue,
we cannot shake the stain of it, the witch hunt will pursue.
and standing all alone, we try to fight the mighty storm,
although we're wet and soaked with pain, as every word is scorn.

The mob and social media condemn with all their power,
and when the law is used, we fall beneath the forceful shower.
Injustice has a habit of revealing dreadful deeds . . .
the might of social mastery will sow some damning seeds.

A nurse, Lucy Letby, was accused of killing babies in the UK and received several life sentences. The shock waves reverberated through law professionals and doctors as they spoke out about the injustice of this conviction. Evidently the hospital failed these babies and she may be innocent. The evidence is mostly circumstantial and it has been pulled apart after the trial. She has appealed and failed and it will probably take years to sort out. In the meantime she is languishing in prison. Is she innocent? Only she knows.

Jealousy

That jealous look of envy had
a streak of painful green,
and witnessed by the victim here,
the bitterness was keen;

no cleansing could remove intentions
written on this face
the eyes were focused, like a lion
sizing up his plate.

A heavy shroud had fallen over
all the charming smiles,
resentment felt inside the bones
can ache for many miles;

destroying joyous compliments . . .
the spitefulness begins,
a menacing black vengefulness
is waiting in the wings.

"Timeless Poetic Verse"

Judas

Loyalty betrayed
by fickle stupidity—
duplicitous rat.

July Heat, a Treat

When someone turned the heat up, I am gasping for some air,
July has now decided to be warm and share its flare.
My plant is now so thirsty that its roots are screaming out,
and even my thin cotton dress is too warm for this drought.

Well, it was me who prayed for sun, I welcomed sunny days,
but now the heat has boiled my blood, I might regret this phase;
I know that it will not last long, the rain will quell the heat,
this weather saps your energy, and I am now dead beat.

In Britain where the weather has a tendency to share
each season in one day, it rains when sun is also there!
And I am glad that finally the ground has warmer vibes,
and out come all the insects, bees and pretty butterflies.

June in England

Why is this month called flaming June?
Today with chilling biting winds--
no sign of heat this afternoon,
no warm hot summer day begins.
How cold it is on English soil--
this land where sunny days are hiding
when skin is yearning for the boil--
to fry beneath the skies igniting!

How warm is my fur coat and hat,
my hands inside my cosy gloves--
they say it's June, and I know that
the mating song is sung by doves.
When will the heat descend on me
and warm my bones, and bleach my hair--
there is no promise, guarantee,
for English weather needs a prayer.

Justice is Served Coldly

He comes across as meek and mild, a victim here of scorn,
although deep down he knows the truth, celebrity has torn,
he had to battle in the court, to prove he was not cruel,
and publicly he set a date, to challenge to a duel.

He then admits he's high on drugs, he drinks, and has a temper,
his Mother, she was violent, and she could not remember--
when she abused her children, and he suffered at her hand,
the evidence, it manifests in empathy, as planned.

And yet he testifies that he would never hit a girl,
as witnesses were silenced, and their texts were never Heard.
The Depth of torture and abuse was hard to hear, or know,
but both of them appeared in court, delivered such a show.

The bottom line is truth will never be revealed to us,
and reading in between the lines, the trial of abuse
has been denied, as fans will raise supportive flags for him,
but he is full of sin, and won't admit his temper's thin.

So once again a woman has to bear the scars of sorrow.
Money, power, following . . . they swagger with bravado--
behind closed doors, brutality is hidden from the crowd,
disguised by actors who manipulate, and disallow.

It's all about who is the master of the social scene . . .
as popularity will paint a picture that is keen,
and justice is the last thing that the public want to free . . .
the mob will hang you easily, as they're too blind to see.

Keep on Writing . . .

When writing words of rage to pages,
loving rhymes to rock the ages,
one thing I've learned, I have to say,
that words don't last . . . they fade away.

No one remembers what you've said,
one night of sleep, your words are dead.
Distractions everywhere we look,
so save your poems in a book.

Once penned, your thoughts will disappear,
and if you save them, hold them dear;
when looking back at thoughts of old,
you read them so they won't go cold.

So leave your legacy behind,
some maybe sad, some maybe kind,
but most of all ensure your word . . .
remain in minds of those you've stirred.

One other thought you need to know,
you might be good in every show,
but once you stop, you'll be a flop,
another writer here will rock.

"Christine Burrows"

Leamington Spa
Where Time Stood Still

An English town in bygone times,
where history is rife,
and living in the past sometimes,
brings ancient things to life.

As All Saints Church sits proud and tall
and overlooks the river,
inside they offer cakes and all . . .
on taste they can deliver.

A friendly, quaint, inviting town,
with tiny bespoke shops . . .
the well-lit gardens are renown
as blooming never stops.

The iron trellis arches add
Victorian reminders . . .
where Royal bands were always grand . . .
a tribute to designers.

The River Leam, a pretty scene
runs though the centre proudly,
in Warwickshire the air is clean--
today it is quite cloudy.

Leave Behind your Message

I leave behind a word or two to wet the eye with love
or challenge with opinion, nudge a heart to look above;
as rhyming poems resonate, and reach the soul inside,
when we identify with words, they tend to be our guide.

In life we suffer from the same annoying little pains,
and memories can bring us grief and leave their mighty stains.
A poem can alleviate, annoy, or just confirm . . .
that all the things we know in life will give us great concern.

A little bit of humour can, begin to quell the storm . . .
a rainbow brings the colour and the sun will soon transform;
the struggle seen in nature, as their battle is so hard,
ignites our passion, letting go of our defensive guard.

In love, in anger, or in war, emotions bring us tears,
as life is full of ups and downs and dreadful taunting fears.
So take a coffee break and open up a book of rhyme--
and soon a soothing wave will calm a racing heart, in time.

"Christine Burrows"

Lift up your Breaking Heart

Stunned are we by some events that scar us all for life,
those memories that never leave, and mark our heart with strife.

Try to let the joy of sun shine on an empty world,
and brighten every corner of our day, so that it's pearled.

Learning over time that life throws spanners with a grudge,
a fair and balanced conscience then becomes our only judge.

Never let the past destroy your future destiny . . .
and free yourself of anxious thoughts, forgiving is the key.

Souls who rule with spiteful, harsh, intentions won't repent,
as they believe, and will deceive, with evil, vile, contempt.

Rise above such wickedness like angels up above,
and fill your world with happiness and much sought after love.

Living in Glass Houses

Entitled in their privilege they have no guidance here,
no understanding, thoughtfulness, a self-centred premier.
It's me me me, not you you you, deceit is rife and kicking,
and they are labelled with a badge, adhered, the logo's sticking.

A rude awakening will soon deliver with a smirk,
those children who think that they should win without the need to work;
the world outside will not relate to those who think themselves
above the crowd, who shout too loud, behaviour here repels.

A humble soul, will have control, and win the bigger prize,
as dedication profits when it slowly gains in size,
and talent can be measured by the tolerance of those . . .
respectful guys, who claim their prize, without the need for shows.

I feel despair for those who care, for silent heroes share,
their efforts leave a trace of human empathy out there;
displays of great compassion will bring shame on those who steal,
as limelight often shines on folk who have no real appeal.

Living in the Moment

My feet sink into sand,
as sea laps over both my feet.
I never thought I'd walk alone,
on shores where we first met,
and yet I know
such moments,
never last.

I blink and time just speeds away,
like shifting sand through fingers,
such memories soon die,
when we are tempted
by the charm,
of other things.

Faces come and go . . .
but nature's scenes are constant.

Never looking back,
as time moves on,
I dwell upon this moment,
take in the sun
and leave behind
my sorrow
and live inside
this peaceful
tranquillity.

"Timeless Poetic Verse"

Love Grows

Love,
it slowly grows and glows within,
and under skin it finds a home;
above all else, we love to win
the love of those admired and known.

The loss destroys our self-esteem
as losing love leaves grief that's keen.

A Peppered Pickle is a poetry form created by the author.

"Christine Burrows"

Love is all that Matters

Nothing mattered in the world, this couple were alone,
into their relationship, they didn't need a phone,
looking into eyes of love and laughing all the way,
never noticing the world around them as they play.

Joyously they loved the company they shared together,
storms and snow could never chill, their love survived the weather.
Giggling, smiling, having fun, and into their sweet meeting,
watching as a stranger, I could sense two hearts a beating.

Pleasing was this scene as these two lovers were akin
doves displaying courtship dancing, rapturous within;
happiness was evident, and it was true and easy,
spirits full of energy as love was given freely.

Lucy Lou Review

Her wild imagination, and inventive on-line posts,
amuse the crowd, her presence loud, upon the site she hosts.
Creative is her humour, and I can't believe how wise . . .
a girl, eleven, is so keen, to change before my eyes.

Her grades in school have reached the heights that everyone admires,
a clever clogs, internal cogs, that smoothly synchronise.
I bet my bottom dollar that she'll make her Mother proud,
when she transfers, and joins the ranks, of scholars that astound.

My biased view will grant this girl, a star for at every turn,
for she is mine, her passion shines, she always wants to learn.
My legacy is in her genes, she is a joy to know,
a treasure dear, my pleasure clear, as I enjoy her show.

"Christine Burrows"

Maintaining Dignity in Old Age

When dogged with slow and clumsy, awkward motion—
as gone are swift and stealthy, youthful signs;
and walking aids encourage our demotion,
when leaning on those sticks with good designs.

When hairs start growing in the oddest places,
and losing same, our heads have been exposed,
our failing eyes, imperfect hearing phases—
will leave us feeling downright indisposed.

Retain your sense of humour in the fight,
as age means there is privilege in wisdom;
be dignified and proud when you are right—
and never let the young destroy your Kingdom.

With ravages of age, we pay the price,
and my advice is read this poem twice!

Making Joyful Memories

We never realise that every day we shape our past,
the memories recorded, as they're always built to last;
accumulating one by one, our history is keen,
to haunt us in the future if we don't adjust routine.

A smile is all we need to take the sting from something sad,
a helping hand prevents a situation turning bad;
our memories are precious, and we need to make them good,
as we recall the past when we become misunderstood.

As now is when we have the chance to gift a word of wisdom,
especially when life is hard and we can't change the system;
and how we deal with tough decisions, helps us see the light,
an optimistic view will give us hope and sweet delight.

Tomorrow we'll recall how we behaved when times were hard,
how cautiously we lived when we were always on our guard;
the moments when our faith and friendship favoured us with stars,
and how we made good memories, that didn't leave sad scars.

"Christine Burrows"

Map Reading

When Patrick decided to travel,
his paper map would not unravel,
it was read upside down,
as he entered the town,
he was a green field full of cattle.

March of the Elephants

They suddenly appeared,
in every corner of the town,
the elephants, for charity,
were colourful, not brown . . .
artistic, brightly styled designs,
unique, and very dapper,
and polished to perfection
painted with a shiny lacquer.

Reminding us to give donations
to the poor and needy,
and not indulge ourselves too much
revealing we are greedy.
This gentle giant has the power,
we believe he's kind,
his silhouette is large as life,
and to the streets assigned.

Large colourful elephants appeared on every street corner, all painted in different designs to make us aware of local charities. They were delightful, and eventually auctioned off to raise money.   Lichfield - July 2024.

Marmalade Hoverfly

A virgin bloom confronts the sun,
and begs the hoverfly to come . . .
at last one perfect Marmalade,
decides to join the park parade.

This delicate winged speedy star,
will dash about inside this spar . . .
and soak up all the morning dew,
its shadow leaves a clear tattoo.

Then others touch this petalled gem,
that's perched upon a shaky stem,
a bumble bee weighs down the cup,
and stops the bloom from looking up.

But when the hoverfly appears,
the flower's fear just disappears . . .
a consummate relationship
where both enjoy a magic kiss.

Memories of Summer

The memories of summer linger when the snow is here,
the lawn's protected by a soft white eiderdown this year;
but I remember picnicking upon that very grass,
in summer when the butterflies can spread their wings and dance.

Today I dream of eating cake with friends beneath the sun,
enjoy the clinking glasses full of fizzy champagne fun;
relaxing in the garden with the smells of perfumed roses,
and gathering the daisies to make pretty perfect poses.

Mid-winter can become a cold and melancholy scene,
and when I see a sign of life, I know it will be spring;
the crocus poking through the snow, encouraging the thaw,
and winter has no choice, as warmer breezes will explore.

My memories will be restored as summer days come back,
my winter clothes are stored, as all my dresses are unpacked;
and summer sun will drench the garden in its rays of heat,
another year I welcome-- summer season on repeat.

Miners

The residue of coal remains upon the skin of miners,
the men who worked the pits, who were intrepid keen survivors,
as dust would settle on their lungs, and blacken with its spite;
this dirty, low paid job, where every shift brought on the night.

And fathers, uncles, brothers, sons, would dig beneath the ground,
despite the risk, the hellish pit, that drew men from the town,
when years of soot inhaled inside would weaken and restrict;
the miners fought to keep their jobs, when coal became extinct.

The picket line where men were in dispute with those who entered,
the pits where many men had died, and some had been tormented,
where scabs would work, as they refused to join the strike campaign,
the coal face was a fearful place, no miners would complain.

For centuries these miners spent their working life in hell,
courageous men whose life was lived inside a coal filled cell,
for hours on end they'd dig and scrape for coal beneath the ground,
no sky of blue, no birds and bees, devoid of every sound.

Missed the Parade

She missed the fine parade because her leaves were much too cold,
and flow'ring was too brave, her leaves were struggling to be bold,
and disappointment filled me with a sense of loss this year,
wisteria refused to bloom and gone was all my cheer.

The cool and bitter temp'rature had chilled the wings of bees,
they hid from winds that blew, refused to pollinate and please.
I waited with anticipation, flowers would not bloom,
in June when they are waiting for some warmth beneath the moon.

Now it is all too late, as spring has had its chance to shine,
wisteria will not display those flowers all in line;
and I still wear my hat and coat to keep my body warm,
my heart is saddened, all because, the sun can't quell the storm.

May/June 2024
The wisteria plant struggled to flower because it was too cold in spring and so the blooms were too weak, and the bees were nowhere to be seen. However, in May, there were many neon blue beetles, because May was warmer than June!

Mob Handed

Disruption, chaos, rioting, can turn to hateful deeds,
as rumour feeds the discontent, that fuels a wicked seed;
and from the maple tree his legs were swinging to and fro,
a rope around his neck, his open wounds are free to flow.

No judge or twelve-man jury passed this sentence here of death,
the mob attacked, and with revenge, they took his final breath.
They hang, they stab, the mob are violent, and use their boot,
with little understanding, or the evidence to shoot.

The victim didn't stand a chance, no words were ever heard,
with no regret, the angry gang dished up what he deserved.
And we are at the mercy of aggressive men who kill . . .
and for these crimes they'll go to hell, they will repay the bill.

Moments Remembered

The empty pool is brisk and calm,
marauders are now silent;
no stains are splashing everywhere,
it's motionless, compliant;
no laughter drifts upon the breeze,
to reach my ears above,
as I look down from where I sit,
and watch a scene of love.

The scene where I once swam a length,
with you so close behind,
the sun would beat upon our heads,
and we would then recline
upon the beds to bathe beneath,
a sun in slow decline,
observe the fading blue turn into
shades awash with wine.

We listened to the blackbird,
serenade us for a while,
and when the bracing night began
to cool the concrete tile,
we hand in hand retreated,
said goodbye to one more day,
in paradise where memories,
once lingered here in May.

Now I return to watch the pool,
and picture what once was,
my memory perfects the scene,
the vision stays, because--
I never will forget your words
that purr between my ears--
"these moments are like magic gifts
that leave us souvenirs".

Momentous Tales

I dwell on loving moments when the embers of the day
remind me that when having fun, the time just slips away.
And what we shared was over in the blink of someone's eye . . .
and memories that linger on, can make us want to cry.

And history falls into books, recorded in a rhyme,
a flash of life within these special years we live in time.
My hope is that my words will resonate in future life . . .
and bring some solace to another person in their strife.

So never let a single moment pass without a word,
recorded on a page so that it can be well preserved,
remembering the love and passion still alive within,
and let your story flow with music in your violin.

Morning Light

The light, it slowly enters in the morning after dark,
I see it try to fight its way through curtains black and stark.
I turn into my pillow wanting more from peaceful sleep,
alas it won't be long before the clock alarm will beep.

Another day is offered as a gift to live on earth
and I appreciate this time, enjoy, for all I'm worth.
The sun comes up and quells the night, and brightens every corner,
despite the rain and cloud above, the day is feeling warmer.

My first thought is, what day is this, my list of jobs is long,
and ticking off commitments, like a battle, makes me strong.
Another day in paradise where life is thriving here--
the privilege of family and friends who bring me cheer.

The light, it slowly enters and another day is dawning,
and birds are tweeting news that we should rise this early morning.
The storm has dissipated, and I pray for sun to shine,
just one more hour of sleep and then this day will all be mine.

"Christine Burrows"

Mourning this Special Sycamore Tree

This sycamore meant so much more to everyone in town,
it grew from roots of timeless beauty— now it's been cut-down;
a stump is all that's left, along the ancient wild frontier,
amid the thriving grass and rock, there is a trace of fear.

How could this tree be targeted by someone with an axe
a symbol of serenity destroyed by this attack.
For centuries this tree has stood, surviving many wars,
and history records a man who felled it without cause.

A spiteful act against the natural beauty of the land,
all words now leave me silent as I cannot understand.
This vandalism marks a troubled mind that should be banned
from seeing skies of blue, incarceration should be planned.

The tree may take revenge by growing shoots of growth anew,
my wish is that the tree forgives this morbid human shrew.
As nature suffers from conceited, selfish, humankind,
who care not for the beauty of our landscape's good design.

This special sycamore tree attracted many visitors to Hadrian's Wall in Northumberland, England. The tree was a magical backdrop for picnics, proposals and vacation photos. An iconic tree that had lived for over 200 years. A timeless image that looked to be a pinnacle of nature's timeless peace.

The tree was cut down by a 60-year old man who vandalised it and reduced it to a stump. This has sent ripples of shock, sadness and also anger around the country that someone should commit such an attack on an innocent tree that had stood for so long and survived many wars. Environmentalists are protecting the stump in the hope that it will regrow over time.

Murderous Machinations

He did not argue with the judge,
as guilt was on his mind,
he knew his rage had tipped the scales,
and he had been unkind.
The hammer that he raised to her,
came down with fearful blows,
now she lay dead upon the bed,
her blood was on his clothes.

The argument had started when,
he could not understand,
why she had slept with someone else,
she said it was not planned.
Betrayal left a scar inside,
and temper rose with hate,
he tried to keep his anger in,
but it would not abate.

Now sitting in a prison cell,
with time to think out loud,
if only this, if only that,
his head in hand, now bowed.
Now broken by his evil deed,
he prayed the Lord would see,
how sad regret had filled his heart,
now he would not be free.

Musical Nights in Spain

In Spain where music feeds the soul,
and feeling whole is paramount;
I count the beats, I'm in control,
and drink Champagne when I go out.

In town where music loudly plays,
I sing and sway to fav'rite songs;
sarongs are worn, the sun's ablaze,
before the drowning night belongs.

The lights are bright the town's alive,
the crickets thrive with slower notes;
the boats are moored and after five,
the shore invites so many folks.

My Grandmama

Her spirit thrives within my veins,
I see her in the mirror . . .
a woman way before her time,
tenaciously, a winner.
When widowed in the prime of life,
the loss was hard to take . . .
but strong, determined, she remained,
there was a lot at stake.

When life was tough, she soldiered on,
no time for gushing tears,
her family were young,
and they relied on her for years.
She gained employment silver plating,
spoons and forks and knives,
the work was hard . . . in this regard,
exuberance just thrives.

I never heard her once complain,
about one thing in life,
despite the hardship she endured,
she never felt the strife.
I'm glad to call her, Grandmama,
her genes are inside me,
she gave to me great power . . .
I still feel her energy.

"Christine Burrows"

My Mog and Me

The mog and me, we are a team, both independent souls,
and when the fog intensely falls we both have diff'rent goals.
The mist makes him invisible, not seeing makes me scared,
he uses instinct like a tool, in drizzle I'm impaired.

But when the sun dries up the fog and I can see ahead,
our roles are thus reversed, as cats are secretive instead.
So each of us relies completely on each other's traits,
I never feel alone when he is watching as he waits.

My cat can catch a mouse, and I can spot a bargain buy,
autonomous are we, and yet our friendship won't untie.
Respectfully we stand alone, each one of us is proud,
but I know we can sense each other, in amongst the crowd.

My Mother

My Mother loved the days of sun,
and in the garden she would run . . .
her sewing with machine would whir,
I see her now in her deck chair.

My Mother loved to sing out loud,
it made her part the heavy cloud,
on days when washing was a chore,
a task that she could not ignore.

My Mother hated washing up,
she left her dirty coffee cup
she much preferred to wind her spool,
creating was so much more cool.

My Mother was sometimes depressed,
and she was not so much impressed
by children who took up her time,
they hindered her when on her climb.

My Mother was a pessimist,
she didn't have a therapist,
and I remember tears were cried,
when she was breaking up inside.

If only I had understood,
and helped her see that all that wood,
had hidden all the pretty flowers,
she only saw wet rainy showers.

Now she has gone, I think of her,
how quickly time stole what we were,
we cannot change what has now past,
my memories are built to last.

My Trip North

I travelled north to find a wealth of kindness everywhere--
a rich and pleasing landscape in abundance here to share.
A place where nature works in harmony with mortal dwellings--
the peaceful rural land where skies encourage new-born fledglings.

The ancient stone and ruins of a bygone age remain--
the footprints of our history, a former English reign.
I walked on paths where many souls had strived to win the day,
and felt primeval ghosts reach out and touch my hair, and play.

The winds of yesterday were whistling through the air up there,
and I enjoyed nostalgia of a long forgotten year.
From Barnard Castle to the Abbey stone at Eggleston,
and Raby Castle, Headlam Hall, beyond comparison.

A small part of the world where time pays homage to the past,
and who would guess that stones this old would still be built to last.
My photographs recorded every step I took up North,
to share these solid silhouettes, and add a little warmth.

And I enjoyed the company of friends who welcomed me,
the wildlife was a joy to watch, the cows would come and see.
For me, a stranger, passing through, I travelled many miles,
a change from city life, and I enjoyed those friendly smiles.

Nature vs Nurture

Impromptu serenade in concert, birds are free to choose,
as there is no conductor, and the dawn is their excuse;
when early morning song is heard, the pleasure is all ours,
we're lucky when our nature flowers here for many hours.

The signs of spring are sparkling in the skies when they turn blue,
the buttercups and daisies dot the scene with their debut.
A season change to rearrange the landscape that we know
and gone are frozen lakes, as sun is melting all the snow.

Although the life outside relies on seasons for its cues,
we watch and learn to navigate a world with diff'rent views,
affected are we by traditions, prejudice and fame,
unequal to our human brothers, though we are the same.

Opinions set out all the rules, unlike our feathered friends,
our status and our right of birth decide our future trends;
if naked in a field, without a single prop or scout,
how would we fare upon the stage, if we were born with nowt.

"Christine Burrows"

New Bags

So many bags on sale this year,
I want to buy them all . . .
and choosing is the hardest task,
though some are far too small.
I might choose black or pink or red,
or maybe blue instead,
I'm tempted by such grand designs,
abundant is this spread.
A bag for going to the prom,
or holidaying in the sun,
whatever the occasion here,
new bags are so much fun!

New Forest Trees

The forest trees resist the breeze,
stand firm against the gust;
and roots provide some guarantees—
to stay upright's a must.

Then man decides to build a house
and trees forfeit their plight,
the roots may die, we have our doubts,
for rights of trees we fight.

And trunks of trees depict the years,
recording all the miles;
I love to see their luscious leaves,
in summer, full of smiles.

The ancient evergreen redeems,
and rescues every heart;
as trees will battle all extremes,
that weather can impart.

New Red Tape

Without a password or a code, I cannot access or reload,
identifying who I am, by image, voice, am I a sham?
Devices reach inside my soul and delve until they reach their goal.
Invasive, stark and downright rude, computers can be very shrewd.

If I default with one wrong key, it won't compute, or trust my plan--
I start the process once again, forgetting who I really am!
To buy a ticket, access funds, I jump through hoops and get the runs!
If I am flustered, get it wrong, the stupid screen will not respond.

The robot in me will not dance, because machines are too advanced,
I'm flummoxed by their automation, questioning my mere creation.
With no ID I will not win, my phone's not charged, my patience thin,
the world is run on coded order, dominating with its torture.

Not long ago I'd wait in line, I'd speak to tellers who had time,
I shopped in stores, I paid with cash, and managers would not harass.
But now I battle with a screen that tempts me to spend more it seems,
and when the goods arrive too late, I battle for a cash rebate.

I long to live for just one day, the good old-fashioned slower way,
to saunter to my local shop, and count out pennies, gossip swap,
and buy a drink without an app, to hail a cab, and use a map.
This automated world is fast, I'd rather live inside the past.

Night Flight

It's Me? I stand, approach with terror,
time to leave inclement weather.
Airports where the process here,
is harsh and cruel every year.
I walk into the lion's den,
it steals my happiness, my zen,
it strips me of all faith and hope,
the airport where I feel remote.

Departures flash, the gate is open,
dashing, thrashing, rapid motion.
Me? I stand, I'm poked and prodded,
do I have drugs in my pocket?
X-rayed me from head to toe,
they even checked my euro dough,
my bags are searched, they took my munch,
I'm not allowed a liquid lunch.

The metal cases clang together,
owners hate inclement weather,
rushing to the planes awaiting,
courtesy is soon abating . . .
Me, I stand, I'm pushed and shoved,
and in the airport I'm not loved,
identifying, checking, sighing,
all those people who are flying.

I'm packed inside a sardine can,
where mice would never be a fan,
but I agree to be enclosed . . .
the doors are shut, the tin can rose,
it flew across the sky at night,
with jet-filled engines full of might,
and Me, I sat and watched the earth,
as to the heavens I am birthed.

"Christine Burrows"

No Fortune Telling

I did not want my fortune told, as I command my life,
in other people's hands I could, succumb to death and strife.
So keep the future sacred, I refuse to see tomorrows show,
if sunshine rays will warm us, or there'll be some heavy snow.

My optimistic view has always silver lined my cloud,
and paved my way with golden paths, where I can sing out loud.
My eye looks deep inside my mind and finds a lucky star,
I ride upon the sparkle, and it lets me travel far.

I'm guided by my inner spirit, laughing all the way,
my pencil writes a rhyming word that keeps me good and gay.
The present time is when I feel alive and flying high,
predicting my tomorrow, would betray my prying eye.

Northern Lights

The Northern Lights came to my town,
and drenched the sky in colour,
the southern borders wore a crown
reminding me of summer--

expanding the Aurora Oval
reaching skies once grey. . .
this vibrant scene is global
as I've heard some others say . . .

they've seen displays in purples,
reds and orange in the sky,
the painted tent encircles
and we never question why.

The activity of the Northern Lights in the northern hemisphere takes place when a band known as the aurora oval covers latitudes of 60 and 75 degrees. This strong activity expands to a bigger area and can often be seen further south in the UK.

Novichok

In silent slippers it will stop
your heart, your soul, your spirit
infiltrate your bones and pop
your brain to mush within it.

The touch of it upon your skin,
will torment every cell
until the serpents sting kicks in
and sends you straight to hell!

The Russians use this tool to send
a message to the West,
this deathly agent is no friend,
a ruthless, evil guest.

The horror of this mean regime
will deaden every thought,
until your brain's completely cleaned
confused and overwrought.

A quick, but painful death will follow,
rot will mush your organs . . .
until you can no longer swallow,
choked by sick contortions.

Putin's tool of terror. Novichok agents are considered more potent than VX gas and they target the nervous system. Death usually occurs quickly. It is highly toxic and can be ingested easily. The Russians use this chemical to kill innocent civilians.

One in a Million

He may be imperfect and often complains,
and sometimes he leaves the odd coffee cup stains.
He cares about others who take up his time,
but when day is done, I know that he is mine.

He hates to be late, and we rush to comply,
when we get it wrong, he is there with a lie;
he gives all his love when we suffer in pain,
he's humble and kind and will not look for fame.

The cat needs a hug, he obliges with care,
if we need a lift, he will always be there.
He smiles and is witty, a joke wins the day,
He's always been there when the sky has been grey.

Our world fell apart when he broke the sad news,
and no one could fill his benevolent shoes.
We miss his kind ways and the jokes that he told,
we hung on his words, they were all made of gold.

"Christine Burrows"

Orange Blossom Bees

The sweet aroma wafting through the warm and sultry air,
has reached my senses, pleasing me, and I am soon aware
that orange blossom petals could encourage all the bees
to wake from hibernation, and display their expertise.

These cheery flowers see the sun and open up with joy,
attracting flying insects to enjoy their fragrant ploy.
But where are bees? I ask myself, when will they join the throng?
I keep a watchful eye, but I don't hear their buzzing song.

If orange blossom, with its scented, scintillating smell,
cannot wake up the swarm and stir the hive where bumbles dwell,
then summer will not be the same without those furry friends,
I only hope they join the show, before the summer ends.

Pacing Time

I did not want to see the sun
fade as the night took hold,
for sunsets make me sad as I
don't like to lose this gold.
I cannot stop the day from ending,
clocking up more years,
and as I age, my inner rage,
turns into bitter tears.

I weep for those I've lost and loved,
I cannot speak to them,
I wasted all my words back then,
this silence I condemn.
the ghosts may haunt and taunt the halls,
but I don't hear their calls,
my dreams restore my memories
behind my bedroom walls.

I wake refreshed to face my day,
I'm grateful I have life,
the clock it ticks too fast it seems,
the speed leaves me in strife,
I savour every minute,
dance and sing along the way,
and try to cram into an hour,
what should take me all day.

Passionate Easter

The passion rises from the ash,
and clashes with all reason;
as Easter facts remind the mass
to celebrate this season.

As we reflect on our beliefs
and see that we are flawed;
a guarantee that we are free . . .
forgiveness is explored.

We make mistakes, we give and take
and rake the ash of time;
for goodness sake, we can't escape
from human, sinful, crime.

We learn from history, affirm,
confirm our dedication;
as we return, and show concern . . .
proclaim our affirmation.

Passionate Release

There was an old codger with plenty of drive,
his todger was fired-up and ready to thrive . . .
as hard as a rock
his wife had a shock
it was ages since she'd had a ride.!

"Christine Burrows"

Peace at Night

The early hours when peace descends,
and on the dark, the night depends--
when people sleep, their noise is silenced,
arguments that could turn vi'lent.

before the dawn when birds still sleep,
and insects take their time to creep,
I can enjoy a world that's still,
no thumping pound . . . pneumatic drill.

Afore the sun wakes up the world,
the night means silence is observed.
I wallow in the peace and quiet,
folk can often start a riot.

Without the chaos, all is well,
I let imagination dwell,
it manifests in words of cheer,
as tranquil moments make things clear.

The joy of early song in trees,
the waking of the bumble bees,
when flowers pray for sun and rain,
the dawn begins with light again.

Peaceful Halloween

I lit the candle, smiles abound,
although the laughter did not sound,
the glow within the pumpkin soothed,
and everyone had changed their mood.

The magic spread, as cats were dancing,
witching hours were soon advancing,
fun and joy had tickled ghosts . . .
no longer did they haunt their hosts.

Instead, the spiders in their webs,
let go of flies and blessed their heads,
the warming soup was hot and sweet
now Halloween is on repeat.

"Christine Burrows"

Pensioners are Sitting Ducks

Too many of you live too long,
becoming far too fit and strong.
Why don't you die and pave the way
for younger kids to have their say.

We'll take away your income here,
and watch you bleed, and make it clear
that you have had a damn good life,
now die, to quell financial strife!

We see you with a brand new car
and hear you play your old guitar;
whilst you enjoy your happy day
we struggle here to make things pay.

But wait a minute, listen up,
We've worked to fill our empty cup,
our labours over many years
resulted in some fearful tears.

We've fought in wars, we battled storms,
and now the calm of peace returns,
so leave us be, as can't you see--
your time will come when you'll be me.

Performance of the Sun flowers

All day is spent absorbing heat from sunny rays that scold—
attracting bees and aphids with their pretty heads of gold.
They bow to sun when it is setting on the earth's horizon,
then waiting for the dawn when rising beams begin to lighten.

In unison the flowers turn, as worship has begun
these sentinels, like soldiers, all obey the rising sun;
not one of them will fail to look, transfixed is every eye,
these yellow petalled faces gaze upon a sunny sky.

The field is dotted with a joyous scene of flowered gems,
and I admire their artistry, their dancing trends with friends,
that gather as a troupe, perform a dedicated feat,
as every flower spins a smile, their eagerness is neat.

Phantom Fog

The ghostly fog clung to the ground,
obliterated all around,
no one could see the way ahead,
and to the roads the mist had spread.

It interfered with aerospace,
no planes could land, or join the race;
it did not clear or disappear,
as cloudy fog was so severe.

The atmosphere was damp and dank,
as scenes in mist were blind and blank;
the echo of a footstep clear . . .
was getting closer at the rear.

When looking out, no one was there,
a phone would promptly ring somewhere,
but visibility was gone,
the frantic phantom fog had won.

Phone Scamming

An unseen hand reached in my purse,
and took a wad of money;
invisible was this damn curse,
I didn't think it funny.

The silent footprint left no trace,
no note was left behind;
the thief without a proper face,
just stole what once was mine.

He hacked into my phone and used . . .
the details there, exposed,
and charges made were not refused,
this theft was unopposed.

An electronic magnet delved
into my private stash,
and cleaned out every cent and yelled,
"I've stolen all her cash!"

"Christine Burrows"

Pink Mallow Bindweed

These tiny trumpets sound their horns,
when spreading pink delight,
across the highlands Mallow Weed
flap petals in my sight;
their floral dancing on parade,
a carnival of colour,
was spotted as they dot the grass,
such splendour, like no other.

Postman's KNOCK

My postman has a mammoth task, his round is far too big,
and when he brings the mail to me, he always has a dig;
too many parcels on his van, and most of them are mine,
he moans about the weight of them, as he is past his prime.

He struggles up the stairs, and when he makes it to my flat,
He's out of breath and weary, will he make it going back?
So close to his retirement, and he cannot wait to leave,
his bag is much too heavy, and I think he is aggrieved!

But I will miss my postman when he gives in and retires,
his moaning and his groaning is amusing and inspires;
an English man who has a plan to ditch his uniform,
another postman bites the dust, because he can't perform.

Procrastination

The haunting starts when jobs are left,
and keeping up will often test,
as leaving jobs around undone,
will bring a cloud, there'll be no sun.

A task that lingers on for days
will grow with urgency, and laze
about with roots that won't give up
until you knuckle down, you're stuck!

The staring eyes of tasks to do
will add to stress and leave in you
a dreaded scar inside your mind
as mounting work can be unkind.

So make a list and then insist
on making plans that won't resist.
You'll have no peace, just be harassed.
until those jobs are in the past!

"Timeless Poetic Verse"

Propaganda

When propaganda spreads its wings
and sings a song of fear,
to try and steer the crowd from things
that should be crystal clear.
The media will lie and cheat
manipulate,
to stimulate,
articulate
with their debate;
create alarm with their deceit.

The Chime Operandi is a poetry form created by the author.

"Christine Burrows"

Pumpkin Puns

When orange pumpkins are for sale,
they will prevail to tell the tale . . .
of diff'rent uses we adore,
when making soup, we ask for more!

When scooping out the pulp inside . . .
displaying pumpkins with some pride,
as candles light up toothy smiles,
we love our pumpkin fashion styles.

The tiny pumpkins, I confess
add magic to my treasure chest,
and I believe that pumpkin pie,
deliciously can please my eye!

The pumpkin farm holds lots of charm,
They're piled up high inside the barn,
together they all laugh out loud,
their spooky look can please a crowd.

And Halloween won't be the same,
without a pumpkin with a flame,
to cheer us in the witching hour,
a warming treat we can devour.

Pure Graceful Swan

She glides upon the surface with a sense of pride-filled joy,
with purest unveiled feathered wings, she's bright, and never coy,
serenity is riddled in her bones, she knows she's prized . . .
her pleasing presence brings delight to me, as I'm baptised.

Her inner grace and beauty, wakes me from internal sorrow,
her spirited commitment and discernment for tomorrow . . .
intuitive, with foresight, she predicts the way ahead,
and leaves a gift for me, as just one feather leaves her thread.

The innocence of swans can symbolise morality,
with virtue and nobility, displayed is dignity;
as I engage with all of them when offering them food,
and thank my lucky stars that I can see this charming brood.

Recollections

I saw *him* standing there like a lost child,
his suitcase in hand, he was leaving.
His decisions were always hurried,
no thought of others, only himself.

Despite my disappointment
I felt sorry for *him,*
that look in his eyes I had seen many times before.
He ran when the heat was turned up . . .
instinctively he always followed the money.

I knew I would not see *him* again,
although I felt grief, I also felt relief,
it was a rollercoaster ride . . .
and I was finally getting off.

I heard he was lonely, living with anxiety,
he never stopped to smell the pretty roses,
or see the sun setting on the ocean.
I reflect on our time together and
pick out all the good times.
I still think about *him.*

Red Veined Darter

A dragonfly passed by my eye,
I thought he was a spy,
he stopped and checked me, I suspect he,
tried to say goodbye.
I can't deny this little guy,
I see when it's July,
will dash and dart, he stops and starts,
adds colour to the sky.

"Christine Burrows"

Reflections of Yesterday

How wistful is the eye when looking back so many years
the longer we are living, common are those dreadful tears;
and joys, they come and go, despite our mounting absent friends,
we try to keep abreast of modern life, and latest trends.

There is no use in wishing life could ever stay the same,
as changes have to be embraced, to stay inside this game;
one day I might refuse to move at speed, I'll slow the show,
it's then I will be labelled as a woman with no go.

When I have lost the will to fight, and stand up for my rights,
I'll hibernate and leave the world to all its darkest nights . . .
inside my little bubble I will live for yesterday,
where nothing matters but the pretty flowers here in May.

Remembering Dean Kuch

Remembering with fondness, my poetic kind old friend,
you battled with your demons, you fought 'till the bitter end;
delighting us with words that I now read beyond the grave,
your spirit still lives on and I remember you, so brave.

The horror that you welcomed, though you scared us half to death,
when we would read your poetry that made us hold our breath!
How your sweet words encouraged me to write another rhyme,
and sadness filled my world when you were dead before your time.

But here I tip my hat to you, and want to spread the word,
your poetry of quality would haunt and could disturb,
you ruffled up our feathers with your words of ghosts and ghouls,
and I enjoyed your talent as you flaunted all the rules.

As you were so synonymous with death and fear and horror,
never were you frightened of what could be your tomorrow,
you taught us all to live for now and have fun with our words,
a tribute to you Dean as you now sing with all the birds.

Dedicated to the late Dean Kuch, fellow poet from
Georgetown Ohio, United States.

"Christine Burrows"

Respecting Thy Neighbour

For those who flaunt the rules, and make a mockery of life,
annoy us to the point that we may suffer bitter strife,
the selfish deed that rides a rough shod boot across our lawn,
with no respect for others, they may damage and transform.

To live in harmony with neighbours, silent rules are shared,
a mutual agreement of respect can be compared
to caring for each other with a touch of warm discretion,
then someone takes advantage and will give the wrong impression.

When owning many cars, the need to park them overnight,
had caused a fight with neighbours, it was not a pretty sight.
The law was called, arrests were made and no one wins the day,
when disrespecting neighbours, there's a heavy price to pay.

Retribution

When those who want revenge, will stop at nothing to succeed,
a kind of hell consumes the mind, and sows an evil seed;
consumed by thoughts of hatred, that no one can satisfy,
until the horror is released, and terror starts to fly.

The storm will shower everyone, and many souls will sob,
the retribution rumbles as a life has just been robbed.
Forgiveness has its roots inside a calm and loving state,
where there is much security, and gone is all the hate.

If only those offended had the time to think ahead,
and reconsider actions long before they go to bed,
the world would be at peace and we would not feel any shame,
alas, retaliation leaves a stain of rain and pain.

Romancing

I may not be in love, but I am open to romancing
I'm moved by song and rhythm in an atmosphere of dancing.
In harmony with passion, when the sun sets on the sea--
an evening filled with music, that will bring a guarantee
that heart's desire to recreate a mood of love on fire,
igniting something deep within, we lovers want to sire.

Embrace the moment, feel the ecstasy rise from the soul,
and be touched by the thrill of lust, to lose our self-control,
arousing sparks of magical, and tantalising movement,
to satisfy and ratify, and bring about improvement.
The aching hunger of a carnal appetite for zeal--
is fundamental to our real existence and appeal.

Royal Blood

Before there was a parliament, some heads would roll on whims,
when looking back at history when we were ruled by Kings.
Accountable to no-one, with an arrogance of heart,
they ruled with ruthless will, as Royal blood set them apart.

The privilege of Royalty no longer has the power,
to judge, condemn, and persecute, and rule us from the tower.
Pomposity, an egotistic attitude was seen
and selfishness, indulgence, is not held in high esteem.

Yet fascinated are we by the Royals and their clan,
we watch and criticise, and I admit, I am a fan.
As through the centuries we've chronicled the ups and downs,
and witnessed bad behaviour of those wearing Royal crowns.

The privilege of birth means that entitlement's not earned,
no skill or talent is observed, yet title is affirmed.
A humble attitude is more endearing to the crowd,
an honest open-hearted view that mystery can't shroud.

"Christine Burrows"

Sahara Sand

Sahara sand, it throws and blows . . .
right up my nose it blocks,
and no one knows why I have chose
to breathe in sandy rocks!

But I will sniff and sneeze aloud
and curse those shifting grains,
as with it brings a cloudy shroud
of sandy dusty pains . . .

I cannot trust, the air is thick . . .
with granules of fine grit;
it covers every single brick
and makes the birds unfit!

Oh Africa your land disturbs . . .
how strong the wind can scatter.
The mighty thrust projects and twirls
and swirls its grainy matter!

San Eugenio

The habits of a sinful life
are evident upon the street,
the nubs of fags are left like strife,
that litter paths beneath my feet.

I see the scars inside their eyes,
the bloodshot trails intoxicate,
as health is sworn to realise
that death is sure to propagate.

The burning pavement hot with stench
of urine left the night before,
as drunks frequent the town and bench,
with no respect for any law.

I walk along and hear the sound
of toxic cars and motor bikes,
a place where no wildlife is found
a concrete town where sin ignites.

The sun may beat, and in the heat,
and bodies burn and burgers churn,
and shops sell trinkets, keen and cheap,
they earn so little in return.

The fake facade where hearts are hard,
and hotels thrive with tourist folk,
the crowded beaches here are scarred
by those who want to drink and smoke.

This is a small resort town in Tenerife, the Canary Islands and it is frequented mainly by the British. They pee in the street after dark and leave cigarette butts all over the place. The locals make money in the local shops selling trinkets. There is an unpleasant smell about the place and the traffic is heavy through the town. It thrives on holidaymakers.

"Christine Burrows"

Sea Dogs

There was an old sea dog from Brighton
who sailed on a boat called The Titan,
the crew were so drunk,
the ship almost sunk,
and walking the plank didn't frighten.

Seasonal Madness

I hear a rustle in the trees,
the season with its sighing tease
can sway the branches, flip the leaves,
Autumnal changes freeze the breeze.
I'm shaken by impromptu chill,
it nips at me, gone is the thrill,
in spring and summer's fickle field,
where floral petalled roses yield.

The damp and frigid atmosphere,
where butterflies now disappear,
commanding skies of greyish cloud,
provide a shroud that's disavowed.
No longer docile, still, serene,
and leaves may fall in this routine,
approved by God's almighty hand,
alarming winds I can't withstand.

The edge of Summer almost gone,
I pray that Autumn hasn't won,
for I still want to wear my dress,
as jeans and jumpers look a mess.
And Autumn means that Winter's next,
and I am feeling very vexed,
the season left us all perplexed,
as summer heat was not expressed.

She Smiles

She smiles, she is congenial, to let the sunshine spread,
to face the world with happiness, as love is in her head;
at work she wears a fake facade, a mask of cheer and smiles,
and no one knows the truth of it, the struggle in her miles.

Nobody wants to buy from girls displaying saddened moods,
so here she is upon the stage, a sparkle she includes;
behind the eyes there is a diff'rent story going on,
but she is here to do a job, so all her grief has gone.

A stranger offers up a smile, and we will trust it's real,
we'll never know the suffering, or know what is concealed
behind a smile there is another story we don't know,
not everyone feels sunshine, people live with ice and snow.

"Timeless Poetic Verse"

Silver Boots

I found a pair of dancing boots
these brutes are hot and sassy,
I love these jazzy kind of suits . . .
to stand out and be brassy!
I saw these silver beauties there,
they caught my eye,
I cannot lie,
I had to buy,
I can't deny,
I sigh with joy, can't wait to wear!

The Chime Operandi is a poetry form created by the author.

Silver Swan

The silver swan moved gracefully,
despite its man-made features,
its metal neck was tastefully
designed by mystic dreamers.
I watched it catch a fish,
and swallow whilst the music played . . .
mechanical it maybe,
but the action it displayed
was magical and whimsical,
delighted everyone,
and even Twain would write
about this shiny silver swan.

This mechanical silver swan is on display at the Bowes Museum in Newgate, Barnard Castle. This life size swan was made in 1774 by James Cox in London. It imitates the behaviour of a real swan as its moveable neck rotates to preen its feathers, and then catches a fish to swallow. It was shown in the Paris International Exhibition in 1867 where it was viewed by Mark Twain who later wrote about it in his book (The Innocents Abroad). I was lucky enough to see it working on 5th July 2024.

Soaked to the Skin

The rain, it tries to wet my head,
I keep it covered, and instead
the drops accumulate, impress . . .
and wet my trousers to excess.

The pelting drops leave heavy stains,
and soak through layers when it rains,
I'm sneezing in the cold and damp,
dishevelled, ragged, like a tramp.

I can't escape the pouring drone
it bores through me to skin and bone
and chills my fervour with its smear,
and nothing now is very clear.

And sun will challenge with its beam
as rain fights back with sheets that teem,
until the sun gives up the ghost . . .
allows the rain to be the host.

I see a weed enjoy the shower,
petals soaking up the power
shooting up with nourishment
and laughing at my punishment.

Then suddenly a bee decides
to whisper words to sun-- confides,
the sun wakes up and dries the scene,
now there's no sign that rain has been.

"Christine Burrows"

Some Never Find Happiness

He never found his pot of gold,
although he chased those rainbows
his dreams of wealth were big and bold . . .
were soon lost in volcanoes.

He never learned to compromise,
or share his love with others,
and finding gold with sombre eyes,
meant he missed many summers.

His self-importance wore us out,
we tired of his obsession,
to loneliness he was devout,
inside his mind . . . depression.

Surrounded by those he had paid,
to do his faithful bidding,
but everyone would be betrayed,
all loyalty was quitting.

He never found his pot of gold,
companionship was absent,
there was no loving hand to hold . . .
his blood was cold and stagnant.

Songs of Love

When early morn delights the birds
with hope their song of love affirms,
at four a.m. I lie awake,
from nature there is no escape.
The rustle of the tree outside,
disturbed by feathered friends inside.

The cooing dove tunes every note . . .
he hopes his love is not remote.

The florid little robin sings,
the chorus of the summer brings
all trees alive with nesting wings,
a day of music now begins . . .
relentlessly the yearning here
is full of optimistic cheer.

The cooing dove tunes every note . . .
he hopes his love is not remote.

Spanish Bureaucracy

Bureaucracy will haunt my soul,
the paperwork is in control;
to miss one sheet, then you are lost
and you will sorely pay the cost.

You take a ticket, stand in line,
and watch your number in decline;
it is your turn to take a chance,
and with the Devil you shall dance.

The Spanish love a paper trail,
and they will fight you tooth and nail . . .
for documents you have forgot,
which means you have just lost your slot.

And round in circles you will go
I'm growing old and still don't know
if I will have success this time . . .
bureaucracy is such a crime.

I'm drowning in officialdom,
a web of tight reticulum;
and those who are successful here,
they leave with loud hell-raising cheer!

Spiked Habit

He stood among the roses,
everyone a perfect bloom,
remembering his youthful days,
he sang a happy tune;
he lit his cigarette and dragged
the nicotine inside,
his lungs were used to drowning,
and the tar was well supplied.

Too late to change direction,
habits never die, but kill,
the very thing that shortened days,
was now his only thrill.
A peaceful aura silenced him,
as he inhaled the spike,
his grave was all prepared, he knew,
that death would surly strike.

"Christine Burrows"

Spring & Summer Life

When Spring and Summer change our scenes . . .
aquamarines
will paint our eyes
with pale blue skies . . .

and lawns of green are rich in fields . . .
blackberry yields,
when sunny days
have long displays.

The nesting birds with early song . . .
their love is strong—
as nature thrives,
within the hives.

A minute Poem

Spring Renews

I braved the biting wind today,
to view the flowers on display;
a treasure trove of colour too,
as every bloom was poking through,
the residue of snowy flakes
that fell upon the fields and lakes,
a frozen, icy day in March,
the ground was solid, stiff as starch.

The air was fresh, no morning dew,
and in the sky, I saw a few
black crows a 'squawking in protest,
the ground was hard, they did their best,
but worms were cosy underneath,
the icy earth had brought some grief,
and every creature prayed for spring,
a hopeful sunny day would bring . . .

new life, new leaves upon the trees,
as bees could buzz inside the breeze,
and birds can claim a nest up high,
and sun would clear a cloudy sky;
as spring is joyful every year,
we hear the pretty songs of cheer . . .
the daffodils and crocus yellow,
buttercups that dot the meadow.

And all in all, a hopeful change
will brighten up and rearrange,
begin again, the cycle runs,
renewing life, as Easter comes;
and I will let the sunshine beams,
allow the rays to shine in streams,
and bathe beneath a clear blue tent,
relaxed is all my discontent.

Spring Serenade

The icy grip relaxes and the ground is soft and moist,
and underneath the surface, I can hear a little voice--
it's asking if it is okay to poke its petals through,
and reach the sky up high, enjoy the sunny days anew.

I see a coloured dot appear and know that spring is here,
a daffodil is full of hope that snow will disappear,
and happily new life injects more vibrant hues around,
we cultivate our gardens, turn the soil inside the ground.

Awakening the bees to pollinate and buzz about,
as Monarchs make their debut, to the blooms they are devout.
No longer are the branches bare, as leaves begin to form,
and nests are hidden from our view, they're sheltered from the storm.

The atmosphere is full of cheer, as spring is in the air,
my favourite place to sit is on old England's garden chair;
I watch the stirring of this season's blooming grand parade,
I'm serenaded by the birds, and welcome their brigade.

Stay Calm

Adversity will foil an easy trip.
An optimistic view will kill the night,
but never let your anger spill or trick.

When navigating mountains, use a stick,
support your journey with that inner fight.
Adversity will foil an easy trip.

Your climb becomes a problem when you slip,
and words spill out, when you are not polite--
but never let your anger spill or trick.

A challenge will reveal what makes you tick,
when darkness falls, there is a lack of light.
Adversity will foil an easy trip,

When pieces of the puzzle will not fit,
frustration boils with temper, you ignite,
but never let your anger spill or trick.

When situations change, and it is quick,
keep calm and never let go of your sight.
Adversity will foil an easy trip,
but never let your anger spill or trick.

A Villanelle

Stealing from Nature

Inspired by nature all around
and every time I touch the ground,
I feel the urge to breathe in life
to quell the chaos and the strife.

But what goes on outside my home
are struggles that I have not known;
the fight within a bird or bloom—
as diligent as sun and moon.

Determination gains rewards,
without the need to draw their swords;
unless a threat presents itself,
then nature screams and it can yell.

Procrastination means they die,
no need to cheat or tell a lie,
no resting on their laurels here,
as nature fights back every tear.

And we should learn a lesson from
the creatures that we come upon;
they work, survive and thrive out there,
we think we have the right to share.

We milk the cow and steal the eggs,
we pick the flowers from their beds;
we pilfer honey from the bees,
and cut down all the healthy trees.

Street Lifers

I see those souls who waste their days,
they laze about in dull malaise;
whilst I fight on, despite the cloud,
if only they could be endowed . . .
with hope to prosper, grab their life,
instead, they wallow in their strife,
and beg all day, and waste their time,
behaviour I think is a crime.

I want to shake them, give advice,
but I know they would not look twice,
they slump into a sleepy trance,
and never change, give life a chance.

My heart, it breaks, to see such waste,
when young men live in such disgrace.
Whilst others thrive, live on the edge
crusading with their life long pledge.
And on their tombstones words are keen,
this man was on the street unseen,
with no achievements to his name,
no voice, no fortune, and no fame.

"Christine Burrows"

Stylish Iris

Oh Iris how I love your smile,
you bring your painted purple sheen—
before I run my final mile
you called me to your floral scene.

Your frilly flags flap in the breeze
you tease me with your ruffled dance;
those leafy veins of colour please—
those tongues in velvet, voice romance.

A quirky blooming blushing trio
petals curling, twirling, fanned;
a vibrant carnival in Rio
never could be quite as grand.

Summer Gardens

I stepped into the garden, as the colours caught my eye,
I heard a bird with cheerful song, in trees as I passed by.
A butterfly then brushed my cheek when fluttering about,
and bumble bees were hard at work, their buzzing had some clout.

The gentle breeze would carry sweet aroma through the air,
the garden bright with pretty blooms had so much flair to share.
I lay upon the rich green grass and gazed up at the sky,
the only cloud I witnessed had decided to stay dry.

The sunny rays caressed my skin, the flowers flaunt devotion,
without the sun, the English roses may not even open.
When summer has the will to bring a hot climatic change,
then every insect, plant and tree, is happy to engage.

"Christine Burrows"

Summer Gardens Speak to Me

My roses have no urgency, they bloom when sun is bright,
and dragonflies will visit them when drawn towards the light;
the bee commands the space, as he weighs heavy on the bloom,
but gentle is his touch, as he enjoys their sweet perfume.

The robins use the branches that have fallen from the trees
to make a nest, they choose the best, to weave them with such ease.
As squirrels prance about as they enjoy my garden's treasure,
the rabbit bobs his tail and sniffs the atmosphere at leisure.

The undergrowth is home to lots of insects on the go
with beetles, ants and snails that seem to know that spring will glow.
as temperatures rise when snow melts deep into the ground,
and once again regenerates my garden's lively sound.

Summer Lane

On Summer Lane the kids played out,
no cars most fam'lies did without,
before the war knocked life about . . .
and bobbies gave the louts a clout.

When crimes were often never seen,
and thugs were always mean and keen,
you'd best be on the winning team,
as no one dared to intervene.

The famous street was talked about . . .
on Summer Lane where kids played out,
as hard knocks made the lads devout
as tough as boots, there was no doubt.

If you were born on Summer Lane,
the legacy would leave a stain,
the city centre thugs explain
that courage, bravery would reign.

"Christine Burrows"

Summertime Joys

A gentle climate soothes the soul
and warms the bones to keep them whole,
as sunny days, with magic rays . . .
in June begin their fine displays.

As flowers open up to sun
and rain has dried, the cloud has gone.
All aphids can now flutter free
in harmony with every bee.

The crows are in a better mood,
and squirrels store their winter food;
the days are long and full of joy
romantic doves are never coy.

I open up my doors to air
and share my secrets everywhere,
no longer am I house confined . . .
I'm free to exercise my mind.

The summer is my favourite time,
in every day I find a rhyme,
as when the sky is blue and clear . . .
I wallow in the weather here.

Sunday Afternoon Driving

When my Mercedes takes a spin,
she clings to corners, she can win,
an open road, with music blasting . . .
Sundays can be everlasting.
Bucket seats, with engine revving,
thrilling, thriving, life reviving,
open country roads ahead,
twisting, turning, pedal red.

This sleek machine is lightning fast,
and every test she has surpassed,
she flies just like a silver bird . . .
I'm changing gear, and now in third.
The open top, exposed to air,
and wind is blowing though my hair . . .
I'm sitting on fine hide upholster
free to ride this rollercoaster.

Sun is setting on the land,
it's time to head for home as planned,
now dark, my motor had some fun,
as she enjoys a good long run.
Tomorrow she will battle roads,
where drivers can behave like toads,
the motorway is jammed with cars,
and I wish I could live on mars.

"Christine Burrows"

Surf the Wave

The wave stood tall and wide with pride,
advancing with its speedy ride,
and mounting on this flushing wash . . .
the surfer to and fro was tossed.

The rapid ride from swish to shore . . .
a thunderous, almighty roar
was heard by passers-by on land,
anticipating sea to sand.

The force would rip and rule the tide,
its crashing, thrashing won't subside.
I saw my girl dive down and deep,
and holding onto life to keep.

The surf is high and in the sky
the Albatross is flying by,
he sees the foolish human kind . . .
obsessing with the ocean slide.

The energy beneath the board,
is pushing, potent . . . power stored,
to harness savage seas at will,
the surfer has to have great skill.

Sweet Revenge

How dare she wear the colour red,
now that her loving husband's dead,
no mourning him for years to come,
embracing life, now he has gone.

The neighbours frowned upon this girl,
too young to give up on her twirl . . .
her happiness was far too bold,
as they believed her heart was cold.

They criticised her for her clothes . . .
this squad of murd'rous jealous crows;
and ostracised her with much scorn,
she didn't have the time to mourn.

They were not privy to the truth,
this man had tried to steal her youth,
controlled by heavy handed plans
now she was free of this man's hands.

A little potion warm and sweet,
administered to make him sleep;
and in the morning he was dead,
no tear by her would then be shed.

Admiring her expensive frock,
in red she gave them all a shock,
with pride she skipped along the road,
toward her peaceful new abode.

The Canarian Storm

I thought I was in England, when the rain fell overnight,
the clouds wept over mountains, and it flushed on through with spite.
It trickled down to reach the beach, and washed it all away,
and cleaned the shores, poured under doors, and flooded with its spray.

Torrential was the tidal flush, it gushed with its abuse,
it washed away the local bridge, collapsing quite a few,
the might of teaming water, would not stop, it was empowered,
cascading deluge taunted, in its wake it soon devoured.

My washing now is soaking wet, I won't forget the chill,
as rain has cooled the atmosphere and drenched the place with skill.
My frizzy hair, beyond repair, was quite a sight to see,
this unexpected downpour was a shock to you and me.

The City Girl Grew Wise

I'd eat my lunch in pigeon park, and reminisce the nights,
those youthful days of long ago, drawn in by neon lights.
The vibrant city moving fast, the theatres and clubs,
I'd eat with friends, wear latest trends, and visit lots of pubs.

The early summer evenings when the saxophone would play,
relaxing by the water, when I'd had a busy day.
As business men in bespoke suits would order pink Champagne,
and office girls would sip and toast, and no one would complain.

The city where the money flowed like honey in the bars,
and smiling glances back and forth, took me to see the stars,
and in the cold and glaring light of day when dawn arrived,
I realised that city life had falsely been contrived.

As secrets shared by loosened tongues would seal another's fate,
the politics, disloyalty, the gossip filled with hate,
I learned to navigate this life, to keep a level head,
I heard conflicting stories, and some bitter tears were shed.

Behind the glossy lipstick of those beauties on display,
lay treachery, and spiteful words intending to betray.
And I escaped the trappings of a life I once enjoyed,
before my heart was torn apart by those who had annoyed.

I now prefer a simple life, with unpretentious souls,
and those I can rely on, those with very diff'rent goals.
Integrity and honesty importantly preside,
within the hearts of those I love, and whom I can confide.

The Final Journey

We see the fate, that life has cast,
and fear what is to come,
will death be painful, will it last,
until we then succumb;
the shroud of permanence will fall,
and take the soul away,
there is no warning when we're called,
as death will not delay.

It will be swift and gift its lift,
to heaven or to hell,
we will not see it coming,
as there is no ringing bell.
But of this I am certain,
it will come my way one day,
that final closing curtain,
that will take my soul away.

The Law is an Ass!

The Crumbleys' tumble to their knees,
no crime committed, if you please,
but scapegoats have to pay the price,
when Governments are not that nice.
At home when cooking up their tea,
their son, with mad activity,
had shot his friends inside the school,
because he thought that it was cool.

The witch hunt then began to churn,
we need our guns, they cannot burn;
society were up with arms,
this incident set off alarms.
The panic is quite clear to see,
it's payback time for you and me,
a mob said: "string the bastards up!"
The parents must be quite corrupt!

And what about the Grandma too,
as she was knitting, this is true—
But she did not commit the crime?
Let's make her do some extra time.
The older sister was at work,
and when arrested, went berserk,
the family are all to blame,
let's hang them all, they are insane.

The Government will search the streets
to find someone they can mistreat.
The rules have changed, the law's an ass!
No one is safe from this morass.
Responsibility should lie,
with Governments, they cheat and try
to put the blame on parents now,
the US law is such a cow.

Are all parents now culpable when their sons and daughters commit murder? When will this madness end in America? This latest law has made me think that the US has completely lost its way. If you can prosecute people for not committing any crime at all, then the US is on a slippery slope down into chaos as it will dismantle the justice system completely. The general population should be in fear for what will happen next. This is a shameful testimony.

The Misery of Rule

When life is on the edge of death, decay will not be long,
our undernourished breath is weak, our body is not strong;
recovery is hanging by a thread of luck and mercy,
without a thirst for extra time, predicted death comes early.

And those survivors know the cost of living in regimes
where mean dictators care for nothing but their own extremes.
Our deeds on earth are witnessed, and we know the price is high,
as cruelty and murder will result in cloudy sky.

The selfishness of man against humanity is real,
compassion has been tainted by a wicked harsh ideal.
Those heroes who take up their swords and fight against oppressors,
are Heaven sent, and championed when fighting these transgressors.

The Mushroom Cloud

The mushroom cloud imploding in the sky
is witnessed by the sun as competition;
the vaporising heat we can't deny—
has brought about a chilling definition.

A planet with the power to deface,
retaliation flattens earthly pleasure;
there is no love or passion to embrace,
or moments spent relaxing here at leisure.

The rain is black, the snow is molten ash,
atomic cloud has blocked the moon and sun;
the ground is burning, life gone in a flash,
and from this bloody threat, no one can run.

The world is ruled by violent contempt,
where no one has the right to live in peace;
discrimination regulates, ferments,
duress will be the number one release.

No heart is won by force, no love is free,
and life is harsh for all those who are weak;
enlightenment is just a memory,
and after World War III, life will be bleak.

The Poet Writes

What drivel has she written, and she got it all to rhyme!
The musings of a poet, pushing boundaries in time . . .
to ruffle feathers, poke the bear and write about the truth.
A dash of sweet nostalgia is remembered from her youth.

And so the page is crowded with those melodies in metre,
created from a mind that won't let syllables mistreat her.
This poet is determined to design a line in verse,
without the need for practice, or the need to be rehearsed.

She spills the beans and has the means to make her inking pen,
scroll words, those pesky verbs are used in time, and time again.
Until a poem sings in tune, she will not let the bobbing moon
distract her from the task in hand, on words she is consumed.

The Puppeteer

He was a clever puppeteer,
controlling all her movements here;
he pulled her strings behind the scenes,
and she obeyed his set routines.

One day she stepped outside the line,
and believed it was a crime;
his temper raged, he lashed with hate,
how dare she cause this big debate.

He put his hands around her throat,
in fear she did not rock the boat,
and to survive she was devout,
and never did she scream and shout.

The years would pass, the fam'ly grew,
and from the start, she always knew,
that life would be restricted here,
there was no love or happy cheer.

She saw a chance to run away,
it was a bright and sunny day;
she packed the kids into the car
and wished upon her lucky star.

He caught her as she tried to run,
and punished with his loaded gun;
the neighbour heard the deathly shot,
she died right there upon the spot.

The Ref

The Ref, he sometimes gets it wrong
and our belief is very strong;
unjustly we have been accused,
the deed will mean our team could lose!

But bide your time when hit by doubt,
as cameras may call him out . . .
the truth is hidden in the proof
as with the ref you're in dispute!

Then suddenly you're in his shoes
and it is time for you to choose . . .
you are Policing on the pitch
decisions made are now bewitched.

So if you're shown a crimson card,
and leave the game cos you've been barred,
don't curse and shout, as this will mean,
you won't be picked for any team!

The Tree Fell Hard

The tree fell hard,
onto the yard,
the wind uprooted it,
and when I saw it lying there,
I wondered how it tripped.

The roots were weak,
and under concrete,
could not spread down deep . . .
now it lies dead and dormant,
Darragh's wind killed it this week.

"Christine Burrows"

The Trial Man

The jury gave their verdict as the trial was complete,
before the judge, he quivered, was unsteady on his feet.
The sentence shocked the court, as shrieks of spiteful shouts rang out,
and broken was this man, who faced a challenge in his life.

The clanging sound of iron bars, locks turned in prison gates,
the halls were filled with hapless men, where loneliness awaits.
Incarcerated in a cell where walls begin to shrink,
as freedom is curtailed, and inmates lose the will to think.

The stretch before him, vast and wide, he cursed his evil deed,
if only this, if only that, regret begins to seed;
with no escape, a cloud descended from the sky above,
in prison, there is only hate, and gone is all the love.

He wore a cap upon his head, his orange suit was bright,
his spirit was destroyed, as he had lost this bitter fight,
devoid of hope, depression drowned his mind, and dogged his days,
where was his faith, as God abandoned men with vi'lent ways.

He found his pen and wrote of his emotional tirade,
alone inside this mean and evil place, he was afraid.
A single ray of light shone on his head through iron bars,
and touched his skin, he felt within, some healing of his scars.

Timeless Poetic Verse

A timeless word can stain the page,
and live forever more . . .
it cannot be removed once it has,
touched us at the core,
as every single syllable,
will tear our soul apart . . .
and whether it is good or bad,
we feel its beating heart.

Sometimes a word repeats inside,
those thoughts we are recalling,
a moment that we treasure,
or despair we are befalling.
A sentiment we hold in time . . .
remember . . . till this day,
those timeless rhymes that sing to us,
and never go away.

Tinnitus

A multitude of engine sounds,
and crashing ocean waves,
the plopping of a constant pain,
a whooshing hurricane . . .
a siren with a pitch so high,
it whistles through my brain,
the pitter patter drowns me
with incessant heavy rain.

The groaning is in both my ears,
alarms that keep on sounding,
disturbing, churning into noise,
that constantly is pounding.
I yearn for silence, peace and quiet,
so that I can rest.
but tinnitus intrudes,
eternal in its mighty quest.

And only when the morning sounds
of early song birds sing,
am I released from murmurings
that pester with their ring.
The buzzing is annoying,

and I'm told there is no cure,
there are some things in life that we
accept and still endure.

Trashy Food

The food they sell is full of trash . . .
as cakes and all the pasties stash
a mix of high fat calories
that drain and suck your batteries.

The process saps the nutrients . . .
infused with salted substitutes;
and added sugar also tempts
addiction to ingredients.

Hot sausage rolls and bread refined,
and sugared doughnuts with design
are coated with a chocolate cream
that give a magic shiny sheen.

The kids will flock to eat this muck,
intestines narrow, food gets stuck,
and starting young forms habits, true,
and soon you're taking tablets too.

Avoid this shop, it has the plague,
as every time you'll have to trade . . .
eat food like this, you'll pay the cost,
a year or two of life is lost.

"Christine Burrows"

Trashy Tash

There was once a cool chef with a tash,
and his whiskers collected the trash,
his girlfriend was keen,
to keep his mouth clean . . .
as he tasted of sausage and mash.

"Timeless Poetic Verse"

Trashy Wedding

When Marcos decided to marry
the venue he chose was quite flashy
too posh for his mates
these punks and no taste . . .
and the bride wore a dress that was trashy.

Tree Hug

When weathering the storms outside,
a tree has roots to make them high,
and standing proud to reach the sky,
their branches spread their wings to fly.

As trees can rustle in the breeze,
they tantalise those nesting bees,
inside their thick and luscious leaves
supporting nests, they sway with ease.

When trees are felled, we mourn their loss,
for when they fall, there is a cost,
for every tree that we adopt—
we save our planet, stop the rot.

Our trees are precious sentinels,
reminding me of generals,
such proud and pleasing spectacles,
that line the streets in festivals.

Extravagantly wild and free--
I want to hug my favourite tree,
they innocently guarantee
to clean the air-- so let them be.

Tree Surgeons save the Day

The trimmers with their clipping sheers
would spruce up every tree,
ensuring all the dead wood clears—
for such a tiny fee.

With ropes and much encouragement,
they climbed up high above—
and after the refurbishment,
the trees would thank with love.

And every year the surgeons come
to cut away the dross,
the ancient oaks and elms have won—
and shake off pesky moths.

Now breathing easy in the park
they stretch and improvise;
without the burden of dead bark,
endorsing their demise.

Trial by Media

The media, where one can rise into a star on stage,
and in an instant all is lost when there are words of rage.
When you can be condemned to death, dismissed by fickle minds,
by those who poke behind a name, and hide behind the blinds.

The frenzy stirs the hornets' nest and stinging is the game,
the media will prod and taunt and you end up insane.
If you expose yourself to it, expect to fall down hard,
as someone finds a flaw, and will exploit you, and discard.

The truth will take some time to be revealed, you sit and wait,
abuse is hurled and tables turned, the onslaught won't abate.
The mob is heavy handed and a lynching will be seen,
as those behind the curtain are disturbing, and they're mean.

So my advice, for what it's worth, is never stand too tall,
pretend to be someone who is much purer than us all,
or tell a lie, or kill a fly, as you will be berated—
a thousand eyes are watching you, and ego's soon deflated.

Trials in Life

Eavesdropping on the early dawn, when rain is beating down,
to wet the earth with water, seeping through the underground;
the peace inside the dark and dull and dank deceptive morn,
brought me a sense of calm to clear my mind, I'll less forlorn.

We cannot change the weather, we accept the rain will come,
the showers soak the lawn and our own troubles often stun;
but peace and rest begin to soothe, when dealing with our fate,
as life is full of obstacles, our paths are never straight.

Our state of mind will need a little help to stay in focus,
to walk without a limp, we need to have a sense of purpose;
striving for perfection has no truth, as life's diverse,
embrace the ups and downs to quell life's troubled, awkward curse.

"Christine Burrows"

Trick or Treat

The night arrived where horror thrived,
with witches, ghosts and ghouls . . .
the terror of this night connived
when creepy creatures break the rules.

The spiders seek to dangle fangs,
their webs will snare us there,
and trick us with their creepy plans,
grow huge and give us such a scare.

But I will peacefully relax,
and watch my pumpkins glow;
I'll sip on soup and eat a snack,
and let the children out there know.

That if you knock my door this night,
a witch will then appear;
and cast a spell, give you a fright,
the magic makes them disappear.

But then again, your luck may shine,
as treats behind this door,
are given out if you're inclined
to trick or treat once more!

Uncouth Wives of Beverly Hills

They're dressed in jewelled dresses, with a coiffured hair design,
stiletto heels from Gucci, and a handbag that's divine,
but when they speak, vulgarity is splashed across the room,
these women are offensive, though they smell of sweet perfume.

Indelicate and common are these ugly, catty wives,
a cocktail spiked with arguments, and out come all the knives.
The crass and common language spouts from mouths that are unclean,
unpolished bar room women with behaviour that's obscene.

The savagery will cut the air, when speaking of their friends,
and open wounds are bleeding as the tirade apprehends.
The decadence is brazen, and the spite will slash with words,
a stabbing frenzy shamelessly begins to cause concerns.

My Grandma used to say that you ca"t hide behind your stride,
a sow is still a sow, a grazing cow has skin of hide,
and etiquette and manners come from learning when you're young—
as no amount of money can wipe clean a serpent's tongue.

Uncovering the Truth

When our suspicions tell us of a truth we cannot see,
deduced from someone's habits, with repeated frequency—
when two and two together calculate an even score,
we open up Pandora's box to find out even more.

The unseen may be visible by making mental notes,
uncovering conspiracy is dangerous for throats!
But once it is confirmed within the mind, it won't abate,
and we will know of someone's fearful, fatal, future fate.

Our eyes and ears are tools that we may use in secrecy,
we watch and learn and soon we can resolve the mystery,
the information gathered can indeed change people's lives
recorded is deceit, unfaithfulness, and big fat lies.

Under the Blue Spring Sky

Beneath the pink umbrella where confetti blooms of Spring
are painted scenes of colour, as the magic's in full swing.
The gentle breeze is waking all the butterflies and bees—
no longer are the trees so stark, they dress themselves in leaves.

I walk beside wisteria, her buds are sprouting fast,
and dotted in among the clover, buttercups contrast.
The cultivated flowers holding on to Latin names,
are often so diverse with beauty, showing off their strains

The flowerbeds with bobbing heads are petalled art in motion,
delightfully they please the city eager for promotion.
The gardeners have worked their magic, tulips in pure white
are everywhere I look, in fact they even shine at night.

The finest welcome home so far has been the cherry tree,
I saw her being planted, now she's smiling back at me;
I haven't seen a butterfly as they are very shy,
but soon I'll greet them all as they will grace this bright blue sky.

"Christine Burrows"

Unladylike Behaviour!

There was once a young lady who farted,
at the Ritz with her friends where she partied . . .
she brought the tone down,
and people would frown,
when the stink from her bottom departed.

Unpredictable Life

When we depend on all those treasured things,
relying on a world we have created;
remember we don't always pull the strings,
be cautious, and expect the unexpected.

Today when clover grows abundantly,
we lie next to a bed of pretty roses,
reforms can shape our world and suddenly,
events can turn when stressful strife proposes.

Our future plans may not come to fruition,
so be prepared to modify and change,
we can't rely on fickle intuition,
some incidents in life can be quite strange.

Our memories are safe when in the past,
when in a happy moment, make it last.

"Christine Burrows"

Vernon's Crusade

When Vernon's vasectomy failure
curtailed his licentious behaviour;
he tied a knot in it,
to stop and inhibit,
and became a French Letter crusader.

Virtuous Spirits

A spirit with a firm foundation,
never fails to please,
morality, sincerity,
can make it feel at ease;
as those who are reliable,
will make so many friends,
when others seek and want to meet
a soul whose love extends,

For we rely on honesty,
to build our hope upon,
for lies, deceit and treachery,
will leave us all undone.
Our history is peppered,
with a trail of hateful deeds,
from Kings to paupers, there are those,
who've planted wicked seeds.

We recognise a kindly soul,
when witnessing their traits,
and often we're inspired,
as their actions resonate.
The heroes of this world,
deserve the highest praise and credit,
so join them when you live your life,
and be someone of merit.

"Christine Burrows"

Vociferous Rage

The anger grew, disturbing was the scene
a mob had gathered, anarchy was rife;
as tensions rose, the men were keen and mean,
incited by their temper . . . threatened life.

Testosterone was high and on the loose . . .
the battle would result in heavy losses,
no words could quell the tirade of abuse,
the fight destroyed the hedgerows and the mosses.

And lay among the flowers were young men,
their blood had covered petals, once pristine,
so short is life when rage can spoil the zen,
and some of them had not reach sweet sixteen.

Regret would tantalise . . . betray,
as shrouds of sadness hung upon that day.

Vulture Culture

Some humans think that we are ugly, some think we are mean;
to put the record very straight, we're here to sweep and clean.
We have an eating etiquette, obey our moral code,
we never snatch or grab at meat when feeding on the bone.

We work the wake, as hierarchy holds the mighty key,
there's nothing quite like meeting up each afternoon for tea;
our loyalty and friendship keeps our band of brothers near,
we are the undertakers of the sky, we have no fear.

Our dirty job is underrated, not for fickle minds
we smell decay from way up high and we have lucky finds.
But rest assured we don't attack or kill a living thing,
and feeding on the dead will keep the landscape fresh like spring.

Walking the Dog

This mutt anticipates my moves,
he lives inside my well-worn shoes,
and knows what I'm about to do,
predicts my mood, my next review.
I glance just once at his long lead,
and there he sits with eyes that plead,
a walk, he guessed was imminent,
as he looks up . . . so innocent.

When out, he is let off the leash,
and he explores, when he's released.
I call him back, he's stubborn too,
and does just what he wants to do!
My stern and low voice tells him no!
But he's too busy, on the go,
he glances back, then runs away,
as he is off with friends to play.

He knows the route through scented smells,
his gift in this regard, excels!
If he could speak he'd list the folk,
who walked this path, all those who smoke.
Those dogs that left behind their news,
he documents the paths they choose,
he's skilled, detecting what's gone on . . .
he sniffs the pong of everyone.

War Torn Syria

A troubled land where harsh command,
would rule the people where they stand;
where leaders murder openly,
and care not that the world would see.

With poisoned gas, the children died,
horrific deaths were not denied,
in fear the people had no chance
to save their kids from this advance.

The mourning leaves a bitter taste,
how can they kill the human race,
those innocents who caused no harm,
such wicked deeds set off alarms.

Destructive men did not debate,
in war torn countries full of hate,
as they enjoyed the killing spree,
returning to their homes for tea.

Corrupt, unholy, evil seeds,
were sewn, and on this habit feeds,
until the mounting deaths repeat,
there is no mercy, or retreat.

The war machine where thugs can thrive,
and it is hard to stay alive,
as some believe that death will soon,
release them from this dreadful doom.

Warring Words Die Hard

When anger flies with fire, and allows a word to hurt,
resulting in a ricochet that rebounds in the dirt.
Our actions change the course of life and sometimes hell breaks loose,
upsetting other people, means we suffer some abuse.

When we decide to make a move, and take a chance in life,
the consequences may be good, or they may lead to strife.
All aspects of decision should be carefully thought-out,
as we reveal intentions, we may also have some doubt.

And in the light of day, we may encounter some regrets,
if we neglect a problem and don't see advancing threats.
as vigilant attention to the details saves the day,
ensuring that we keep the peace, will pave a safer way.

"Timeless Poetic Verse"

Water Striders

With hydrophobic legs,
these skaters skim across the pond,
they glide above the water, never think.
The surface tension will not break,
with no connecting bond,
and so these striders never ever sink!

They feel the water moving,
balance weight and flex their feet,
above the water, moving in their cliques.
The colony, will cleverly,
perform their daring feat,
their wizardry, enchants us with their tricks.

Water striders use high surface tension to walk on top of the water. Their hydrophobic legs mean they do not break the water's surface as they balance their weight evenly and flow with the water movement. How very clever.

"Christine Burrows"

What Makes Someone a Hero?

Those selfless acts in times of war,
some punch above their weight;
compassion we've not seen before,
these men and women state:

"I don't think I'm a hero here,
I did my job, took care of others . . .
on this frontier, watch your rear,
provide the back-up for your brothers".

But those who go beyond their role,
and take a step into the mire . . .
when saving others on the whole
as death, the risk, when under fire.
The spirit of heroic folk . . .
when faced with threats of danger . . . fight,
despite the bullets and the smoke,
they always see the shining light.

Heroes are compassionate humanitarians with empathy, and will risk their own life, and face of danger, to save others.

This is dedicated to Hiroshi 'Hershey" Miyamura, (1925-2022) a Japanese American Staff Sergeant, who was awarded The Medal of Honour after his contribution to the Korean war. He single handedly held off a Chinese attack against overwhelming odds on 24th April, 1951, so that his men could escape capture. He survived, and spent 27 months in a POW camp before being released.

When Looks Can Kill

A look can speak a thousand words,
destroying faith with its absurds,
contempt is faxed, intentions clear . . .
when thoughts are hidden, looks will steer.

And instantly we know the score,
our heart beat rises, tensions soar;
the eyes can bore, the message sent,
and peace is broken . . . venom vents.

This silent, mighty, bulletin,
without a sound begins to win,
a scowl can indicate a fight,
and with its power, kill the light.

This knowledge we can't argue with,
conveyed by eyes that won't forgive,
the threat of consequences rife,
controlling eyes don't need a knife.

Windy Days

The gusts that blow and snap the trees
are more than just a passing breeze!
They wreck the palms that lose their charm,
as gushing wind promotes alarm.

And white sea-horses flash on beds,
as boats are forced to forge ahead;
the speed is rapid, to and fro.
they battle with the hellish blow.

My hat takes flight, my buttons pop
my coat is now just flying off!
I feel the power lift my hair
and throw me up into the air.

The aftermath of this destruction,
caused by windy mad disruption—
debris litters every town,
and everybody wears a frown.

Winter's Menacing Chill

The trees are well prepared for winter's chilling icy frost,
and birds that stayed at home know there will be a heavy cost;
as gentle snowflakes fall and form a layer thick and strong,
and temperatures drop as snowmen never melt for long.

And even when a cloudless sky begins to bless the day,
the sun will never warm the ground with its hot potent ray.
As seasons have command upon the earth this time of year,
and nothing stops the drift of snow becoming more austere.

But I will view the scene behind my double glazing glass,
where I am warm and cosy when the wind performs its blast;
and if I venture out, I have my fur lined boots and hat,
although my cat refuses to step off the comfy mat.

My ageing bones may ache, as flesh is thin, without some meat,
and soon the ice will penetrate, to freeze my bony feet;
I pray for spring to bring some colour to this scene of white,
and praise the purple crocus when it searches for the light.

"Christine Burrows"

Youthful Fashion Trends

A fashionable vape with diamanté sparkling spout,
was put into her mouth, she drew on nicotine for clout.
The smoke descending from her nostrils, something she enjoyed
This small, petite young dragon had a frown that looked annoyed.

Big hoops hung from her ears, a sturdy bolt propped up her nose,
her legs were covered in fragmented, knotted panty hose.
Her mini skirt did not quite cover all of her essentials,
and when she tied her laces, she revealed her rear credentials.

Her lashes almost swept the pavement, long and thick with black,
her long and straggly hair extensions made a stark impact.
Her personality was larger than the busy town,
and when she walked along the street all heads would turn around.

Youthful Memories

I walked along a childhood path, I saw the past so clear,
such memories of long ago were singing, dancing here;
the games we played, the friends we made, now gone without a trace,
who knows what happened to them all, they left an empty space.

Relying on my recollections, filling in the gaps,
I see my long lost friends right here, my visions are enhanced.
The wonky skates, and wobbly bikes, the broken scooter too,
we made the most of life outside, the sky was always blue.

The happiness within our souls projected fun and laughter,
and friendship was the key to all and nothing else would matter.
Those carefree younger days back then, where freedom felt so good,
we all went on our separate ways, now everyone's matured.

The Author's Biography

Christine was born in Birmingham, in the United Kingdom, where she has spent most of her life. Her passion and love of poetry started at college when she was lucky enough to have her first poem published, 'The Beach', at the age of seventeen. Since then she has developed her talent for rhyming words, and many more poems have been published on 'Amazon', 'Forward Poetry' and 'The United Press'. Her poems have also won contests on Fanstory.com. She is pleased to present this book called Timeless Poetic Verse.

Other recent poetry books include:

'Steadfast Sonnets'	-	160 Shakespearean Sonnets
'Dickens' Characters in Rhyme'	-	Full Colour illustrated Poetry Book
'Seasonal Delights'	-	Full Colour illustrated Poetry Book
'300 Soulful Sonnets'	-	300 Shakespearean Sonnets
'Glimpsing Light in Poetry'	-	500 Poems with b/w illustrations
'101 Poetic Personalities from History'	-	A full colour book of famous faces
'A Plethora of Poignant Poetry'	-	200 Poems with b/w illustrations
'The Fascinating World of POETIC Bugs'	-	100 Poems with full colour illustrations
'The Poetic Philosophy of Life'	-	130 Poems with b/w illustrations
'POETIC Bird Watch'	-	A full colour poetry book of birds
'POETIC Flowering Blossom'	-	A full colour poetry book of flowers
'The Awdl Sonnet'	-	Dedicated to the Awdl Sonnet Form
'I Dream in Sonnets'	-	Introducing the Awdl Sonnet
'The Awdl Gynt'	-	Poems dedicated to a welsh poetry Form

All available on Amazon.com

Christine originally worked as an aerobics fitness instructor for local authority gyms around Birmingham, and also Aston University, before retiring.

The inspiration for this book comes from personal experiences of love and loss, emotions, reflections and challenges in daily life and the influence of politics in this ever changing world. The challenges in our changing weather has manipulated our environment and we need now more than ever to find inner peace and calm with good thoughts and a positive attitude for the future. Admiration and appreciation for others, including wildlife, enhances one's feeling of well-being. The joys of life are free, if we just open our eyes to them. My muse enjoys the pleasure of life itself, the power to survive is strong in all creatures on earth.

Welcome to: Timeless Poetic Verse

Nature Inherits the Earth

Among the ash there sprouted up a lonely leafy green,
from deep beneath the soil, a root was eager to be seen;
it grew past devastation, never noticing the drought,
with hope, determination, Mother nature sends her scout.

The tiny plant then grew and sucked the nutrients below,
ignoring all destruction on the surface full of woe.
The flat and lifeless land was silent, cloud was thick and grey,
but in between the cloud the plant had glimpsed a sunny ray.

No human life was left, the plants inherited the earth,
and slowly trees were reaching skies, enjoying their rebirth,
an unhatched egg had movement and a chick broke free from it,
a bird would learn to fly, and soon a song would bring a lift.

The harmony of nature, where all living things abide . . .
no conflict unresolved, as every living thing had pride,
and earth was soon a place of peace, the meek were in control,
the lambs were shy and docile, lions bowed to their parole.

The lesson that was learned where human kind paid with their life,
was compromise, forgiveness, would have taken all their strife.
Alas, it was too late, they had their chance to rule the world . . .
but selfishness and greed was what all nature had observed.

MMXXV

Printed in Great Britain
by Amazon

11e1deb4-1d55-4e71-ac8b-817f79dde827R01